Walk!

Mallorca

with

Charles Davis

DISCOVERY WALKING GUIDES LTD

Walk! Mallorca
ISBN **9781904946953**
First published January 2014
Reprinted April 2016

Copyright © 2014, 2016

Published by Discovery Walking Guides Ltd
10 Tennyson Close, Northampton NN5 7HJ, England

Maps
Maps sections are taken from
Walk! Mallorca Tour & Trail Super-Durable Map
ISBN **9781904946977** by **David Brawn** for Discovery
Walking Guides Ltd

Photographs
Photographs in this book were taken by the author,
Charles Davis, and Jeanette Tallegas.

Front Cover Photographs

Cala Corbó

Capelleta de Santa Maria

Orient from the *mirador*

Cala Castell

ISBN **9781904946953**

Walk! Mallorca

CONTENTS

THE WALKS

EXERTION GRADE ONE WALKS

EXERTION GRADE TWO WALKS

EXERTION GRADE FOUR WALKS

EXERTION GRADE FIVE WALKS

Charles Davis is the author of numerous books for Discovery Walking Guides and has also published several novels. For full biographical details, blogs, and news of forthcoming publications, see:-
www.redroom.com/member/charles-davis

Published by
Discovery Walking Guides Ltd

Walk! The Alpujarras
ISBN 9781904946878
Walk! Andorra
ISBN 9781904946045
Walk! The Axarquia
ISBN 9781904946656
Walk! Brittany (North)
ISBN 9781904946359
Bumping About Brittany
ISBN 9781904946441
Walk! The Cathar Way(PDF)
ISBN 9781782750109
Walk! The Costa Blanca Mountains
ISBN 9781904946854

Walk! Dorset
ISBN 9781904946205
Walk! The Lake District (South)
ISBN 9781904946168
Walk! La Gomera
ISBN 9781899554904
Walk! La Palma
ISBN 9781904946687
GR221 Mallorca's Dry Stone Way
ISBN 9781904946489
Walk! Mallorca (North & Mountains)
ISBN 9781904946496
Walk! Mallorca (West)
ISBN 9781904946700

Other Walking Guides (Santana)

Costa del Sol Walks
ISBN 9788489954397
Costa Blanca Walks
ISBN 9788489954571

- and novels, by other publishers:-

Walk On, Bright Boy
ISBN 9781579621537 Permanent Press
Walking The Dog
ISBN 9781579621674 Permanent Press
Standing At The Crossroads
ISBN 9781579622138 Permanent Press
Displaced People
ASIN: B00B26LG54 (Kindle)

INTRODUCTION:- MALLORCA IN THE MIND

"If you're at your wits end, or think you are, which amounts to the same thing, if you're dazed and confused by the noise of civilisation and the haste to get someplace where you find you have nothing to do, if busyness has swamped your brain with facts and science blinded you with gimmickry, then follow me to an island where calm reigns, where the men never hurry and the women never age, and even the sun and the moon move at a more leisurely pace."

So begins 'La Illa de la Calma', Santiago Rusiñol's Belle Epoque celebration of Mallorca. Perhaps the men move a little faster nowadays and doubtless the women age like everyone else, but the need for respite is more acute than ever and, happily, Rusiñol's evocation of tranquillity is as true today as it was a century ago, for Mallorca remains a haven of stillness and beauty blessed with a remarkable capacity to enchant.

One shouldn't necessarily trust numbers, still less celebrity, yet when such disparate figures as Boris Becker, Jorge Luis Borges, Richard Branson, Pierce Brosnan, David Cameron, Frederic Chopin, Agatha Christie, Michael Douglas, Harrison Ford, Stephen Fry, Ava Gardner, Robert Graves, Goldie Hawn, Grace Kelly, Kate Moss, Anais Nin, John Noakes, Jamie Oliver, Michael Palin, George Sand, Claudia Schiffer, Michael Schumacher, Freya Stark, Andrew Lloyd Weber, Bradley Wiggins, and assorted royalty choose to spend anything from a season to a lifetime in a given place, there must be something going on that's worth investigating. A more mismatched assembly of fame would be hard to imagine, yet all have found a temporary or permanent retreat in Mallorca . . . and this the island that was once a by-word for mass tourism.

Woods above Valldemossa

There are, of course, other places popular with both privileged elites and package holidaymakers, but Mallorca is distinguished by a knack for absorbing outside influence without losing its distinctive personality, a faculty that has as much to do with the ingenuity and adaptability of its people as the gifts bestowed on the island by nature.

Tranquility - La Muleta from Cala Deià

The Balearic Islands get their name from the Greek word for slingshot, a weapon the original inhabitants employed to such deadly effect that they were permanently identified with it and earned a place alongside the elephants in Hannibal's army. They owed their facility to a custom whereby the food of young Balears was placed in the uppermost branches of tall trees. If they couldn't knock it down with a slingshot, they did without. This uncompromising training produced an ingenious people who understood that if you didn't adapt to circumstances, you went hungry. It's a message that has been passed down through the generations, shaping not just the island's economy and the character of its people but the very landscape itself.

approaching Coll d'es Pi

On Mallorca, mountains that would elsewhere have been dismissed as a wilderness best left to misfits, hermits and bandits were prized as a refuge from invading armies and marauding pirates, who were so prevalent that the coast is dotted with watchtowers built to warn of their arrival.

Lavadero at Biniaraix

On Mallorca, a topography any sane plains-dwelling farmer would tell you is too precipitous to be cultivated was portioned out, scored with terraces, enclosed by some of the most improbably perpendicular walls you will ever see, and turned into valuable farmland. On Mallorca, tiny niches in otherwise impenetrable cliffs were dubbed 'ports' and transformed into focal points for fishing, communication and trade. On Mallorca, even the most inhospitable terrain was home to hundreds of families whose painstaking labour progressively traced out the tracks, trails, and paths that are now one of the island's most vital resources.

the Archduke's Path

When agriculture went into decline and poverty loomed, Mallorcans concluded that if one could no longer export the fruits of sunshine to wealthy foreigners, one must import wealthy foreigners to the fruits of sunshine.

Thus, at a time when the inhabitants of Torremolinos and Tossa del Mar were still mending their nets and reckoning the cost of another pair of rope-soled sandals, Mallorcans came up with the bright idea that one could sell such intangible and apparently unpackageable assets as light and heat, and set about inventing mass tourism. And then, when environmental radicalism was promoted to orthodoxy and everybody agreed that mass tourism wasn't necessarily an unparalleled Good Thing, it was Mallorca that pioneered the shift up-market to quality holidays and eco-friendly tourism, reinventing itself as Europe's most popular warm island walking destination.

ON THE GROUND

As with so much that is praiseworthy in Spain, we have Africa to thank for the Balearics, which are in effect the exposed tip of the Baetic Cordillera, squeezed out of the earth's crust during the middle Tertiary period when pressure from the African plate occasioned all manner of happy havoc along southern Europe's tectonic frontiers. Subsequent folding, faulting, and karstic erosion have moulded this raw material into a tormented landscape of sheer cliffs and deep sinkholes, weirdly fluted rocks, razor sharp ridges and fissured limestone pavement.

What nature provided man has perfected, dappling the austere rockscape with groves of olive, almond and orange trees, taming precipitous slopes with neat terracing, canalising springs and streams, building remote mountain farms and beguiling sanctuaries, and gathering in picturesque fishing hamlets and atmospheric villages, all of which are linked by a complex network of paths pioneered by farm-labourers, muleteers, pilgrims, charcoal-burners, lime-firers, and snow-gatherers.

Blue seas: Cala de Deià

The last three are particularly important for us, as these were the rural industries that penetrated the more inaccessible corners of the island, leaving their brand not only in paths but in the form of *sitjes*, circular moss-covered charcoal hearths, partially interred *hornos de calç* or lime kilns, and *casas de nieve* (*casa neu* in Catalan) or snow-pits.

Es Cornadors

The variety of walks on Mallorca is remarkable, ranging from gentle strolls down peaceful country lanes and alongside idyllic aqueducts, through energetic hikes on cobbled donkey trails to pathless scrambles up wild mountain tops.

Walking in Mallorca, we wind through pine forested slopes above azure blue waters, enter narrow gorges with towering walls that nearly touch high above our heads, peer over gratifyingly frightful precipices, marvel at dizzying sea views, discover secluded creeks where swimming seems not so much desirable as compulsory, encounter rock formations so artfully sculpted that you'd swear they were carved by hand, and admire olive trees so old and gnarled that George Sand compared their contorted forms to fairytale monsters, while Rusiñol got so excited that he spoke of "such hysterical convulsions they can hardly be called trees; they are more like epileptics"!

Sunset over Dragonera

The best known walking area is the **Serra Tramuntana**, the range of mountains running along the north of the island, where we find Mallorca's highest summits and deepest gorges. The key destinations within this range are **Valldemossa**, **Deià**, **Sóller**, **Cúber**, and **Lluc**. **Valldemossa** has been luring outsiders with an eye for a view ever since the fifteenth century, when the Carthusians petitioned King Don Martí to let them settle in the old royal palace. The monastery is there to this day, perched on a pedestal of higgledy-piggledy terraces and surrounded by carefully manicured trees, but for our purposes the principal appeal of this area is the **Teix** massif and the legacy of a latter day visitor, the fabulous bridleway known as **The Archduke's Path**.

The Archduke's Path

Cami d'es Correu, above Banyalbufar

East of **Valldemossa** and perhaps best known as the former home of Robert Graves, the village of **Deià** has become one of Mallorca's most prestigious resorts, its spectacular location and exquisitely preserved atmosphere appealing to both well-heeled walkers and a bewildering variety of celebrities.

But the most popular base for walkers is **Sóller** and its port, which draw in the vast majority of visitors on a dedicated walking holiday thanks to the central location, good facilities, a fine selection of local walks, and ready access to the high mountains. The name **Sóller** comes from the Arabic for 'a golden shell', which is a suitably evocative description for this fertile valley, where a passion for horticulture has saved the land from being carpeted with tower blocks, as it would have been in most other areas of Spain.

Sa Dragonera - from La Trapa

Climbing into the dramatic rockscape of the high mountains beyond **Sóller**, we come to **Cúber**, a picture postcard reservoir girded by mountains and some of the island's most famous walks, after which we descend past the **Torrent de Pareis**, Europe's second largest gorge and a favourite with canyoning enthusiasts, to reach the monastery at **Lluc**, a place of pilgrimage that is in many ways the spiritual home of Mallorca.

In the northeast, the **Tramuntana** peters out behind the old towns of **Pollença** and **Alcúdia** and their respective ports that now double as beach resorts.

Bucolic landscape of the south - above Esporles

But the drama is not done yet, for beyond the beaches lie the mandible like headlands of **Cap de Formentor** and the **Alcúdia Peninsula**, the first of which is stippled with a succession of sail like summits, while the second is fringed by spectacular rocky promontories. By contrast, in the south and west the **Tramuntana** tapers into a bucolic landscape of tightly clustered villages flanked by sun-dappled woodland and framed by the intermittent spines of impressive limestone escarpments.

Pas Vermell

ON THE PAGE

To help you explore this walkers' paradise, our latest book about the island draws upon the three previous publications, Walk! Mallorca West, Walk! Mallorca North & Mountains, and The GR221 Mallorca's Dry Stone Way (an LDP running the length of the island), to give a

comprehensive overview of walks from **Peguera** and **Calvià** in the southwest to **Alcúdia** and **Pollença** in the north-east, including all the principal walking destinations in between. Walk! Mallorca West and The GR221 Mallorca's Dry Stone Way are recommended for those who, in the first instance, don't intend visiting the main stretch of the **Tramuntana**, or, in the second instance, aim to follow the GR as a long distance route. For the general visitor, though, and for those based in the main walking destinations and the resorts in the northeast, Walk! Mallorca features all the classic itineraries plus a few rarities for people who already know the island reasonably well. The main body of the book is taken up with walks classified by exertion rating organized from west to east within each section. The final section features stretches of the GR that would be suitable for day long linear hikes using public transport and, in one case, for a two day walk with an overnight stop at the **Tossals Verds** refuge.

ON THE WEB

In order both to remain up to date and to leave more space for walking routes in the book, Discovery Walking Guides are in the process of putting more and more ancillary information online. This is an ongoing project, but for GPS data, updates, background information, other readers' experiences and (hopefully, in time) alternative itineraries, check out:

http://www.walking.demon.co.uk/mall.htm

ON THE CALENDAR

Given the fierce heat of summer, September to May is the walkers' season in Mallorca. Autumn and Spring are best for birdwatching, April and May for lovers of wild flowers. Winters are generally mild and dry, though snow is not impossible. If you're relying on public transport, schedule your trip for May or September.

ON THE MAP

The map sections used in this book are developed from the new Walk Mallorca Tour & Trail Map Super-Durable version. For each walking route the map section is aligned with North at the top of the page and the waypoints for that route are added so that you will not confuse the route with other walking routes in that area.

Digital editions of Walk Mallorca Tour & Trail Map are available for use with **Viewranger** and **MyTrails** gps apps on 3G phones and editions are available in kmz file format for use in **Google Earth** and **Garmin** mapping gps units. More information on page 18.

If you have the Mallorca North & Mountains Tour & Trail Map then our On The Map Appendix on page 153 explains the correlation between the 'Walk Numbering' in Walk! Mallorca and our other Mallorca titles.

DWG's Symbols Rating Bar gives you the key information about a walking route in a quick glance. Remember that effort/exertion and refreshment ratings are the author's opinion and the time shown is walking time without stops.

our rating for effort/exertion:-
1 very easy   **2** easy   **3** average
4 energetic   **5** strenuous

approximate **time** to complete a walk (compare your times against ours early in a walk) - does not include stopping time

approximate walking **distance** in kilometres

approximate **ascents/descents** in metres
(N = negligible)

 circular route    **linear** route, out & back    **linear** route, one way

 risk of **vertigo**   **refreshments** (may be at start or end of a route only)

Walk descriptions include:
• timing in minutes, shown as (40M)
• compass directions, shown as (NW)
• GPS waypoints, shown as (Wp.3)

MAP NOTES & LEGEND

The map sections used in this book have been taken from Walk! Mallorca Tour & Trail Super-Durable Map (ISBN 9781904946977) published by Discovery Walking Guides Ltd.

All map sections are aligned so that north is at the top of the page. In the interests of clarity adjoining and inter-linking walking routes have been deleted from the map sections for each specific walking route. Waypoint positions, and numbers, refer to the walking route that the map section is illustrating.

ALTITUDE & FEATURES

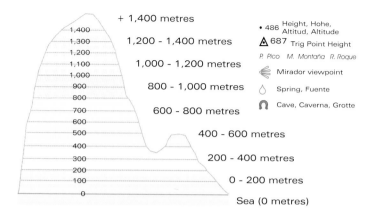

+ 1,400 metres

1,200 - 1,400 metres

1,000 - 1,200 metres

800 - 1,000 metres

600 - 800 metres

400 - 600 metres

200 - 400 metres

0 - 200 metres

Sea (0 metres)

• 486 Height, Hohe, Altitud, Altitude

△ 687 Trig Point Height

P. Pico   M. Montaña   R. Roque

Mirador viewpoint

Spring, Fuente

Cave, Caverna, Grotte

ROADS, TRACKS, TRAILS

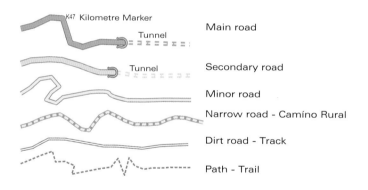

K47 Kilometre Marker

Tunnel   Main road

Tunnel   Secondary road

Minor road

Narrow road - Camíno Rural

Dirt road - Track

Path - Trail

Walking Routes

Walk Mallorca Route (Red)

17   GPS Waypoint
5   see Waypoint Lists

GR221 route in green

Important House   Hotel   House   Ruin/Barn   Tower

Petrol   Bar/Rest   P Parking   Information Office   Church

Lighthouse   Chapel   Picnic area   Cemetery

Sports Ground   Camping   Wind Turbine

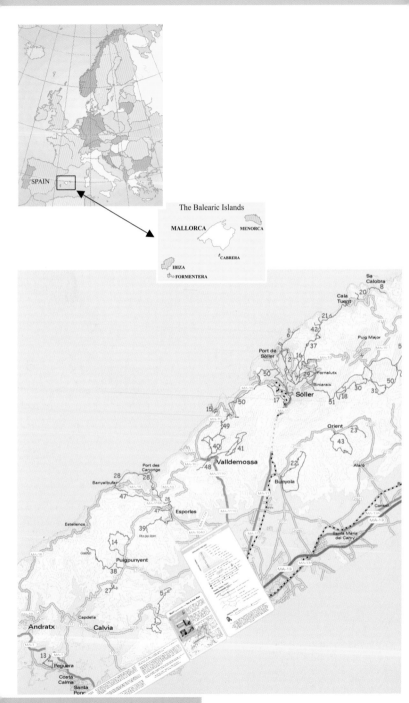

Location maps, and detailed maps accompanying each walk in this book, have been adapted from:-

Walk! Mallorca Tour & Trail Super-Durable Map
ISBN 9781904946977

- published by **Discovery Walking Guides Ltd**.

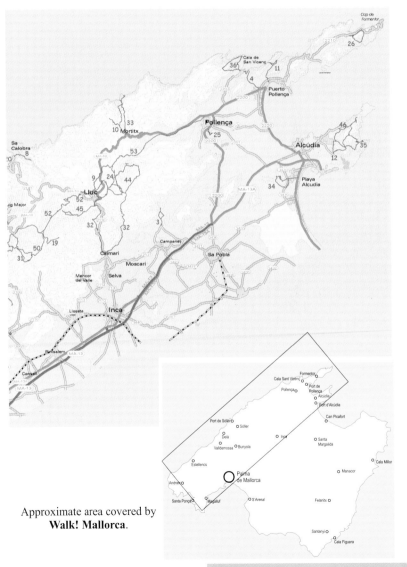

Approximate area covered by
Walk! Mallorca.

As the pioneers of using gps for walking navigation, we are often singing the praises of the pin-point navigational accuracy that you get by using a gps. However, all the routes in Walk! Mallorca are accurately described so adventuring on our routes is simply a matter of following the walk description.

A gps might not be necessary but will always be useful if you want to know exactly where you are on a walking route. If it's your first time on Mallorca then a gps will be useful in finding the start of each walking route; with the walking route's waypoints loaded in your gps, simply activate the 'Go To' function for Waypoint 1.

All the waypoints for our Walk! Mallorca walking routes are available as a free downloadable zip file. Locate the download page on our website, then download the zip file to your hard drive, unzip the file and you will have all the individual waypoint files in gpx file format; then simply load the files you want into your gps or phone app.

If you are thinking of a gps for your walking navigation then our GPS The Easy Way introduction to gps walking navigation is available as a free download in pdf format from DWG's website:-

www.walking.demon.co.uk

Digital editions of Tour & Trail Maps, including Walk Mallorca Tour & Trail Map, are available.

If you have a 3G phone, we suggest you look at the gps apps by **MyTrails** and **Viewranger** who supply digital editions of our Tour & Trail Maps for their apps which enables you to use your phone offline as a full mapping gps unit without incurring any phone call or roaming charges. For more information see their websites.

Discovery Walking Guides publish digital editions of Tour & Trail Maps in kmz file format for use in Google Earth and with the Custom Maps function of Garmin mapping gps units such as eTrex20/30, Oregon, Dakota, Montana. Individual Tour & Trail Maps are being made available for purchase as digital downloads.

A collection of all the digital Tour & Trail Maps plus all the gpx waypoint files that relate to those maps is available as a CD from booksellers. Whether you choose an individual digital download, or the Collection on CD, the combination of top quality digital mapping at DWG prices make these maps the best value in digital mapping.

Tour & Trail Maps (2014) in **Custom Map (kmz)** digital editions, plus the gps waypoint files from **DWG's Walk!** books for those **Tour & Trail Maps**.
Published by **Discovery Walking Guides Ltd**
Copyright © D A Brawn January 2014
ISBN 9781904946991
all rights reserved

Often neglected by ramblers, the **Serra de na Burguesa** between **Calvià** and **Palma**, is a lovely area for gentle walks with fine views. Though most of the forest along the ridge has been destroyed by decades of fires, the eastern end still boasts some fine pine woodland interspersed with a host of bushy strawberry trees - the red-skinned, orange-fleshed fruit is edible but a bit bland and floury. These woods are also home to a tremendous number of songbirds that conspire in a dawn chorus so intense it sounds like an avian parliament debating a particularly contentious point of order.

Despite the dryness of the highlands, the walk is sufficiently easy to be a pleasant evening excursion during Summer, climbing to the *mirador* for the sunset (take your aperitif!); needless to say, it's equally agreeable as a half-day outing throughout the rest of the year.

Access: by car. The walk starts on a green-gated dirt track (Wp.1 0M) at km 6.4 of the PMV-1043, which is marked with kilometre and 100-metre posts, so there's no need to set the odometer. If you have a very small car and a delicate turn of the wrist, there's one parking space beside the gates (do not park in front of the gates as these tracks may be used by firefighting vehicles), otherwise there's more room 150 metres up the road and, beyond that, at the **Coll des Vent** (see Walk 5 for a link path from **Coll des Vent**).

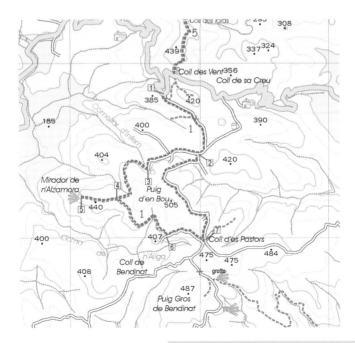

From km6.4 of the PMV-1043, we take the green gated dirt track (Wp.1 0M), ignoring a minor branch on the left near the start (alternative access from **Coll des Vent**) and climbing very slightly through attractive woodland with good views of **Galatzó** (Walk 38) and **S'Esclop**. The track crosses a belt and braces chain against unauthorized traffic and is joined by another track climbing from **Coll de sa Creu**.

Seventy five metres after the junction, we turn right on a minor branch heading west (Wp.2 15M). Ignoring overgrown branches to left and right a little over five minutes later, we continue in a westerly direction between a dense hedging of strawberry trees. The track then descends to the south-west, crossing a dry water course, the **Comellar d'Infern**, and passing a lime kiln (Wp.3 25M), after which it dwindles to a trail.

After climbing across a sparsely forested rise, the trail levels out above **Pla d'en Palem** and follows a contour line round **Puig d'en Bou**, crossing land devastated by forest fires and now almost exclusively colonized by cistus, *Pistacia lentiscus*, and asphodels.

Superb views of S'Esclop and Galatzó from the *mirador*

At a junction (Wp.4 35M) within sight of **Cap Andritxol** and the telecommunications masts and turquoise firewatch tower above **Vilarrassa**, we maintain a westerly direction to the ruined cabin at the **Mirador de n'Alzamora** (Wp.5 45M), from where we have superb views of the high peaks to the north and the bucolic plain behind the coast.

Retracing our steps to Wp.4, we bear right to circle **Puig d'en Bou**. The path descends slightly before curving east and dropping down to cross another dry watercourse, after which a gentle, southerly climb on a gradually broadening trail brings us to a T-junction with a track into the **Coma de n'Aliga** (Wp.6 65M).

Turning left, we climb to a second T-junction, this time with the main track along the ridge (Wp.7 75M). Turning left again, we cross **Coll d'es Pastors**, ignoring two tracks branching off to the right. Defined by sheets of gladioli, the main track climbs along the southern side of **Puig d'en Bou**, levelling off after five minutes at a rare vantage point taking in almost the entire length of the **Tramuntana**, from **S'Esclop** in the west to **Massanella** in the east (Walk 45). We now simply follow the main track through a long gentle descent, rejoining our outward route at Wp.2 (100M).

A gentle stroll on quiet country lanes, dirt tracks, and ancient cobbled ways, ideal for a day off when you still fancy a breath of fresh air. Despite the proximity of the beach resort and holiday homes, this is still very much working countryside, as you will see if you happen to be here in autumn when stacks of sacks of carob pods line the terraces awaiting collection. The route is clearly sign and wayposted throughout.

*very gentle inclines

Access: on foot from **Sóller**. To reach the start from **Sóller's** central **Plaza de sa Constitució**, take **Carrer de sa Lluna** next to the BBVA bank, then second left on **Carrer de la Victoria 11 Maig**. Go straight on at the crossroads and bear right at the bridge (signposted 'Piscina Municipal') into **Avenguda d'Asturies**. The football ground is on the right 150 metres later.

From **Sóller** football ground (Wp.1 0M), we follow the 'Port Sóller' road for 100 metres, forking left just after the **Club Petanca** (Wp.2) and taking the middle tine of the triple fork 300 metres later (Wp.3 8M), heading toward a church with a distinctive square tower. Carrying straight on at the church (Wp.4 11M), we leave the town behind as we stroll along an increasingly narrow and attractive lane leading to the MA10. Crossing the road carefully (cars whip round the bend at a hell of a lick), we follow the **Finca Can Penya** lane (Wp.5 18M) for 150 metres, then fork left into **Camí de sa Pages** (Wp.6).

After passing in front of a row of terraced houses, we climb along a cobbled trail that feeds into a track which we follow for 175 metres (NW). When the track bears right behind a house, we fork left on a wayposted path (Wp.7). The path crosses then rejoins a dirt track (Wp.8 40M) on which we maintain direction (N) for a gentle climb to the **Coll d'en Borrassar**, where we carry straight on at a Y-junction (the left hand branch) (Wp.9 44M) and remain on the track at the junction with a signposted path descending to the left 50 metres later (Wp.10).

the terraced houses

stacked sacks of Carob pods

We now simply stay on the main track, passing **Can Alfonso** (orange juice available) and enjoying unfolding views of the **Balitx** massif, until we reach the MA2124 (Wp.11 63M). Turning left, we follow the road for a kilometre and a half down to the roundabout at the northern entrance to the new **Port de Sóller** tunnel (Wp.12 80M).

tunnel of a different order

Turning left, we follow a signposted trail shadowing the tunnel access road. Just before the tunnel entrance, we pass a tunnel of a different order, and our path veers left to climb through the woods. Ignoring a cairn-marked shortcut, we stick with the wayposted path, zigzagging up across retaining walls amid delightful woodland to reach a boundary wall (Wp.13 90M). The path runs alongside the wall then

view of Ofre & Es Cornador

goes through a couple of gates before rejoining our outward route at Wp.10 (99M). We return the same way with the option of staying on the dirt track at Wp.8 and following the **Can Penya** lane back to Wp.6.

NB For an interesting alternative ending (discovered by chance after we had finished our main research) follow the **Can Penya** lane then turn left 200 metres before Wp.6 on the **Camí de ses Alzines** dirt track (signposted with a blue plaque on the wall) (Wp.Alt1).

The *camí*, which becomes a path during the middle section, emerges 500 metres later on the MA10 beside the **Sa Teulera Restaurant** (Wp.Alt2), from where we simply cross the road and follow the **Camí de ses Argiles** and the **Camí de Can Domatiga** to rejoin our outward route at Wp.3.

3 CAMPANET: FONTS DE UFANES

The **Fonts de Ufanes** are ephemeral springs that flow after prolonged periods of heavy rain in the highlands (to check if they're in spate, call 900151617). However, water is not the only attraction to this tiny itinerary. The woods of the **Gabelli** estate, where the springs are situated and which has recently been purchased by the government, are so enchanting that this is a lovely stroll even without the fonts. Ideal when it's too hot or too overcast to venture into the mountains. Apart from the diversion up the torrent, the itinerary is clearly wayposted throughout.

Access: by car; the **Gabelli** estate lies NE of **Campanet** which lies SW of **Pollença** and can be reached via the MA13, MA2131, and MA2132. From the northern end of **Campanet**, take the **Camí Vell de Pollença** to **San Miguel** chapel, where the walk begins. This point can also be reached via **Camí de na Pontons**, which is the continuation of the MA3421 north of **Sa Pobla**. If approaching from the northeast, the **Camí Vell de Pollenca** can be joined from near km47 of the MA2200.

charcoal burners' hut

We start from the picturesque chapel of **Sant Miguel** to the east of **Campanet** on the **Camí Vell de Pollença** (Wp.1 0M). Strolling back to the road, we follow the Cami Vell for 75 metres to a tiny wooden gate giving pedestrian access to the **Gabelli** estate (Wp.2 2M), where a broad track traverses an idyllic pastoral landscape. Taking the left fork at a Y-junction (Wp.3 10M), we soon leave the grazing land and enter the woods, which are some of the loveliest in the public domain. Immediately after passing a particularly fine reconstruction of a charcoal burner's hut, we fork right at a Y-junction (the branch on the left ends at locked gates a couple of hundred metres later) (Wp.4 20M) to approach a large *casa forestal* that functions as an information centre.

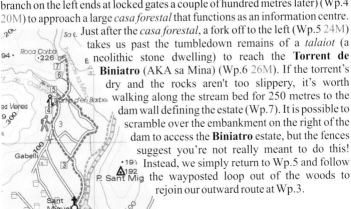

Just after the *casa forestal*, a fork off to the left (Wp.5 24M) takes us past the tumbledown remains of a *talaiot* (a neolithic stone dwelling) to reach the **Torrent de Biniatro** (AKA sa Mina) (Wp.6 26M). If the torrent's dry and the rocks aren't too slippery, it's worth walking along the stream bed for 250 metres to the dam wall defining the estate (Wp.7). It is possible to scramble over the embankment on the right of the dam to access the **Biniatro** estate, but the fences suggest you're not really meant to do this! Instead, we simply return to Wp.5 and follow the wayposted loop out of the woods to rejoin our outward route at Wp.3.

This simple traverse of the low lying hills between **Port de Pollença** and the quintet of creeks that make up **Cala St. Vicenç** is one of Mallorca's classic strolls. Previous publications by Discovery Walking Guides featured a slightly more adventurous version of this itinerary, but unfortunately the alternative paths are increasingly overgrown, so for the present we can only really recommend the straightforward linear route.

Access: on foot from **Port de Pollença** or **Cala St. Vicenç**. From the seafront in **Port de Pollença**, we take the **Pollença** road (**Carrer de Joan XXIII**) and turn right at **Bar Juanito**, 20 metres before the ELF/Cepsa petrol station, on **Carrer de Cala St. Vicenç** (Wp.1 0M). Crossing the new bypass, we take **Carrer de les Roses** to the left of the beige house with blue shutters. Ignoring four branches on the right, we follow **Carrer de les Roses** into open countryside before turning right to head for **Elcano** boatyard.

At the quadruple fork between the boatyard and the 'L'Hort de Siller', we carry straight on along a well-stabilized track. When the track swings left into a private house, we continue on a rougher dirt track. When this track also swings left (Wp.2 15M), we bear right on a broad walking trail. The trail climbs gently at first, then more steeply as it narrows to a path, which runs into a dirt track, 150 metres from a water-hut on the **Coll de Siller** (Wp.3 25M). After the coll, we ignore all branch paths and simply follow the track down to a large surfaced roundabout (Wp.4 40M).

Taking the second exit to the right, we follow the road down to **Cala Corbó**, the first of the four creeks of **Cala St. Vicenç**. We return the same way.

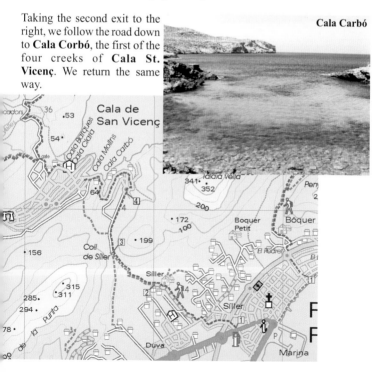

Cala Carbó

Though the **Serra de Son Camps**, a low line of hills defining the junction of the **Valldurgent** and **Puigpunyent** valleys, is virtually unknown to outsiders, it's a little like the local country park for outward bound residents of **Palma**. In the good-old bad-old days, it was a favourite place for dumping obsolete sofas and defunct fridges, but now that the countryside is regarded as a life-enhancing resource rather than an unusually robust rubbish tip, the debris has largely been removed, the tracks have been closed to motorized vehicles, and the only wheels you're likely to see up here will be on a mountain-bike.

The climb to the firewatch tower on **Pujol des Gat** (Hillock of the Cat) is a straightforward linear walk that gives great views of all the major summits at the western end of the **Serra de Tramuntana**. The itinerary can be extended (see 'alt finish') to incorporate Walk 1 for a full day's outing.

Access: by car; the walk starts from km 9.3 of the PMV1016 (**Calvià** to **Establiments**) on a dirt track closed to traffic by metal gates carrying a '*Coto Privado de Caza*' (private hunting) sign. The 300-metre post is on the right behind the fence. Parking's tight here, there's room for two small cars, but larger cars may have to go 500 metres uphill to park safely. If this is the case, note that there's a stretch of dirt track on the right just east of km 8.9 and a path just east of km 9.1 to diminish the road walking.

The gates are locked and lateral fencing blocks access to vehicles on either side, but a well worn route at the eastern end of the fence takes us on to the dirt track (Wp.1 0M), which immediately passes a narrow path climbing to the right. Throughout the ascent, there are several minor branches off the main track, but we ignore them all, and simply turn right at each major junction. The track climbs steadily (ENE), soon bringing the distinctive, triangular summit of **Galatzó** (Walk 38) into view off to our left (NW).

After passing the ragged teeth of a decayed lime-kiln, the track gradually bears right (SSW) and the gradient eases as we climb past a small *aljub* or water-reservoir above the shallow, wooded gorge of **Sa Coma Bella**. The track then levels off amid more varied and healthier woods, interspersed with the abandoned fields of the **Rota de Son Camps** - *rota* being a local word (very local, even people from **Palma** don't always know what it means!) for a mountain smallholding with a cabin rather than a full farmhouse.

After passing a broad grassy trail on the right, the track crosses a wall and climbs gently to a narrow cross track (Wp.2 25M) where we bear right.

From this track we have more good views of **Galatzó**, to the right of which low cliffs define the summit of **Es Puntals** (Walk 14). The small town below **Es Puntals** is **Puigpunyent**. To the west of **Puigpunyent**, the wooded massif with several large houses near the top is the **Fita del Ram** (Walk 39).

After a long, level stretch lined with oak, honeysuckle, cistus, and bushy strawberry trees, we pass a second, better preserved lime-kiln.

Ignoring a trail branching to the right immediately in front of the lime-kiln, we resume our steady climb to a second major junction (Wp.3 35M), at which point we again bear right.

We now climb onto the main ridge, catching our first glimpse of **Palma** bay. The track climbs, levels and climbs again, bringing into view the firewatch tower on **Pujol des Gat**.

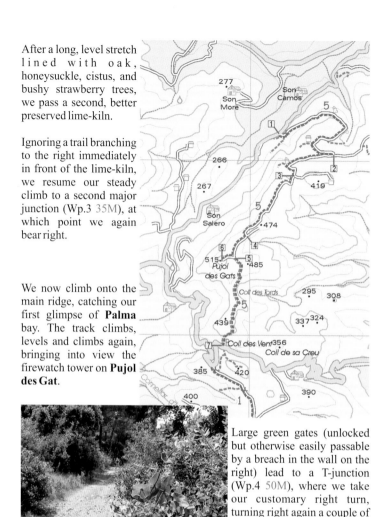

Honeysuckle on the long, level stretch

Large green gates (unlocked but otherwise easily passable by a breach in the wall on the right) lead to a T-junction (Wp.4 50M), where we take our customary right turn, turning right again a couple of hundred metres later (Wp.5 55M) for the final climb to the top (Wp.6 60M).

We return the same way, but if you want to make a full day of it, bear right at Wp.5 and follow the clear trail (rough and steep at first, but soon becoming smoother and less steep) till it ends at the **Coll des Vent** just north of km 6 on the PMV1043 (Wp.7 75M). Ten metres to the left, a trail continues to the south. At the fork 20 metres from the road, turn right on a broad trail descending to join the dirt track fifty metres from the start of Walk 1.

This is the ultimate picnic walk, climbing to the **Torre Picada** watchtower above **Port de Sóller** for coffee and biscuits, then following a lovely corniche path to a *sitja* below the **Puig Balitx** cliffs for an aperitif, before finally descending to a superb look-out point over **Sa Illeta** island for the main picnic - come prepared! A good family walk.

2   3¼ H   **   14 km   250m / 250m   out & back   0

** + 20 minutes for the **Punta Larga** extension

Access: on foot from **Port de Sóller**. From **Port de Sóller** sea front, we take the road toward the new tunnel next to **Hotel Generoso** (Wp.1 0M) into **Avenguida 11 de Maig** and **Carrer de Belgica**.

After a steady climb, the road swings sharp left (Wp.2 10M) and we maintain direction on a narrow tarmac lane. The lane climbs steadily then steeply between olive terraces before swinging sharp right at the **Coll d'es Figueral** in front of a gate and stone wall with steps over it (Wp.3 20M). For our coffee break at the *torre*, we cross the wall and immediately turn left onto the cairn-marked path between the trees.

The path climbs gently, passing several shortcuts, before emerging on a dirt track just below a T-junction backed by mounds of rubble. Taking the right hand branch of the T, we climb the broad track till it dwindles to a trail leading to the **Torre Picada** (Wp.4 30M) from where we have fine views along the coast and inland. On the nearside of the tower, a trodden path leads down to a grassy platform that's ideal for our coffee break. To return to the *coll*, we retrace our steps and, 75 metres after the stone gateway to the tower, where the trail widens to a track under the pines, bear left on a narrow, waymarked path. Rejoining the main track lower down, we bear left again and follow the track back to the *coll* (40M).

We now continue along the tarmac lane, which soon levels out, bringing us into fine views of the **Penyal Bernat** pinnacle and **Sa Illeta**, and passing a sign for 'Es Coll des Ille, Privat', shortly after which the tarmac ends and we continue on a dirt track.

... to pass below a cabin ...

After a tight chicane, a cairn indicates a shortcut climbing across the terraces to our right (Wp.5 55M) and re-crossing the dirt track higher up. At the second junction with the dirt track, we bear left to pass below a cabin. We now continue along the dirt track, passing the idyllically situated and well-restored main house and several satellite cabins.

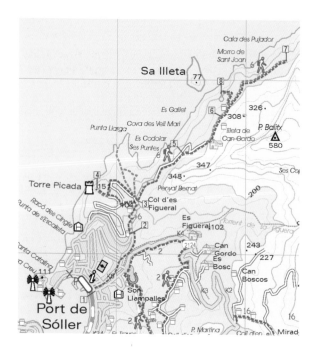

Shortly after passing the drive to **Can Bardi**, we come to a locked green gate where cairns to the right indicate a way through the fence above the gate (Wp.6 70M).

We then walk along a retaining wall for 20 metres and, ignoring the main trail that continues through a wall-gate with a stone hinge bracket, bear left to descend through another gap in the wall, just after which there's a Y-junction of paths. The branch on the left is the way down to our picnic spot, but for the moment we continue on the main path, descending gently through the woods. The path comes into fine views of the cliffs below **Es Joncar** and passes a slightly vertiginous stretch before ending in a *sitja* (Wp.7 90M), just in time for an aperitif. (N.B. The waymarked routes continuing from this *sitja* both involve some precarious scrambling and are <u>not</u> recommended.)

Refreshed by our aperitif, we retrace our steps to the branch path just after Wp.6 and take the lower path descending steadily on a slippery carpet of pine needles to a stand of half-a-dozen water barrels fed by a spring (Wp.8 125M). After eating our fill and gazing on the great crocodile's snout of **Sa Illeta**, where hundreds of seagulls swirl overhead like swarms of midges, we return by the same route.

If you want to bathe on the way back, take the narrow path descending north from **Coll d'es Figueral**. (It's possible to make a loop using the broad track heading NE, but this doesn't add much and is only recommended for those wishing to while away an afternoon exploring the headland). When the path comes into a slight rise, soon blocked by fallen pine, bear left and follow the gully down to a lovely little inlet, ideal for rock-bathing in calm seas.

This pleasant short walk follows two classic cobbled trails climbing towards the **Mirador de ses Barques**. Despite recent wayposting, these routes are little used nowadays, which is a pity as they provide a perfect introduction to the peaceful countryside around **Sóller**.

Extension	Stroll
To the **Mirador de ses Barques** and **Port de Sóller** (see Walk 16).	To Wp.4 then descend via the **Costa d'en Flassada** path, which arrives in **Sóller** a little way north of the football ground.

Access: on foot from **Sóller** From **Sóller**'s central **Plaza de sa Constitució**, we take **Carrer de sa Lluna** next to the BBVA bank, then turn second left on **Carrer de la Victoria 11 Maig**. Carrying straight on at the crossroads, we fork right at the bridge (signposted 'Piscina Municipal') into **Avenguda d'Asturies**. At the football field 300 metres later, we take the **Fornalutx** road, which we follow for 200 metres (Wp.1 10M).

When the road crosses **Pont de Can Rave** beside a 'Camina per Mallorca' mapboard, we turn left on a tarmac lane. Ignoring the concrete track 150 metres later (Camí de ses Marjades), we turn left 50 metres further along onto the **Camí de sa Capelleta** (Wp.2 15M). The path climbs behind two houses and crosses a dirt track. At a second junction with the track, we bear right and, 100 metres later, turn left to recover the path.

We then cross the track three more times before joining the final stepped ascent (briefly interrupted by the track) to the **Capelleta de Santa Maria** (Wp.3 27M). The chapel is a nicely proportioned building and benches outside provide a pleasant spot for a breather, though the interior is chiefly remarkable for its egg-box wall (NOT a metaphor!).

Capelleta de Santa María

Continuing our ascent from the chapel gates, we cross the MA-10 onto a clear well-marked path that climbs steadily, occasionally alongside, occasionally crossing a concrete track before joining the **Costa d'en Flassada** path (Wp.4 35M).

Bearing right, we continue climbing between terraces, coming into fine views of the **Mitx Dia** on our right.

At the next junction with the concrete track, we bear right to recover the wayposted path 30 metres later. Steady climbing brings us to another signposted concrete track (Wp.5 45M) where we join the descent of Walk 16. Bearing left (in the direction of **Port de Sóller**), we contour round the mountain, following the track as the concrete gives way to dirt. After 500 metres, the track swings right, climbing through another concreted section (Wp.6 55M).

For the **Mirador de ses Barques**, bear right and follow the waymarked walking trail visible just above us (Walk 16 Wp.2). For **Port de Sóller**, bear right and stay on the track. Otherwise, turn left to descend the initially grassy then cobbled path between terraces.

After going through a gate and passing a small spring, the path runs into a track descending to a large farmhouse (**Can Nou**), just below which we bear left, off the tarmac driveway, onto a grassy path marked by blue arrows (Wp.7 65M). Going through a light wire-mesh gate, we recover the cobbled trail and cross more terraces. After a sturdier metal gate, we continue our steady descent down to the MA-10.

Crossing the road, we take the concrete driveway down to **Can Bisbal**, where a final cobbled stretch leads into a concrete and tarmac lane (**Camí Vell de Balitx**), which ends at a T-junction with the **Camí de Son Blanco**. We turn right at the T-junction, then left at the next T-junction and follow the **Camí de ses Argiles** back past the football ground and into **Sóller**.

The **Torrent de Pareis**, Europe's second largest gorge and Mallorca's most challenging adventure excursion, is conventionally approached as a linear descent from **Escorca**. However, the full canyoning experience is sufficiently adventurous to elicit complaints that it is inappropriate in a walking guide, so we developed The Old English Sheepdog Trial, reasoning that anywhere we could go with an Old English Sheepdog, others could follow unencumbered. Whatever your company though, this is definitely a place to visit and there is every likelihood that this short outing will be one of your most memorable excursions on Mallorca.

To avoid the crowds, arrive early or late; above all avoid the road down to **Sa Calobra** at midday, when it's chocablock with coaches. Do not venture into the gorge if there's a risk of rain or the rocks are wet. Even in dry conditions, take care on the smoother rocks where there's only one way through: so many people have passed, the rocks are not so much polished as burnished. There is no reliable GPS reception in the gorge.

*in **Sa Calobra**

Access: Sa Calobra can be reached by car (an extraordinary drive in itself), boat (from **Port de Sóller**), and bus (L355 from **Alcúdia** and **Pollença**). Since most people will probably be arriving by car, we start our walk from the main car park at the end of the MA2141.

Descending from the **Sa Calobra** car-park, we bear right onto the promenade (0M), at the end of which we go through two dimly lit tunnels onto the pebbly beach at the bottom of the torrent, where we bear right, heading toward the interleaved walls of the gorge.

The gorge gradually narrows and, next to an emergency-services sign, we come to a permanent pool (20M).

To the left of the pool, we clamber through a natural tunnel formed by an immense rock and the canopy of a fig tree, after which the rocks get bigger, the walls get taller, and we get smaller.

Passing a second large fig tree, we cross a slab of rock, after which we start boulder-hopping and squeezing between massive sculpted rocks. At an immense rock (30M) almost completely blocking the way, the trail appears to bear left, though this in fact ends at a large pool.

We bear right to scramble over the rocks. 75 metres later, we bear right again, passing under a looming cavern onto a 50 metre flat stretch leading to the next jumble of boulders (38M).

Following the clearly burnished trail, we climb across the middle of the rocks, and approach the narrowest section of the gorge, marked by a distinct menhir-like rock (43M).

The beach at Sa Calobra

The gorge narrows even more, the cliffs climb higher, we continue shrinking. Passing a dripping mossy rock with a small fig tree sprouting from its centre, we squeeze to the left of a long low rock virtually blocking the gorge. Climbing over (under if you're the dog) a final boulder (150-200 metres after 43M) we come to a 'ladder' of boulders, where you may find a knotted rope (50M). Dogs don't do ladders. We return the same way.

Though it features no outstanding summits or spectacularly wild corners, this is a very easy and very pleasant introduction to the karst and woodlands around **Lluc**, visiting the famous **Camel Rock** and crossing an astonishing rock garden.

| 2 | 3H | * | 11.5 km | | 200m / 200m | | 3 |

* Short Version 50M (estimated) ** in **Lluc**

Stroll: to the **Camel Rock** and back.

Access: by car or bus (L330 from **Palma**, L354 from **Alcúdia**, **Pollença**, & **Sóller**, L355 from **Alcúdia** and **Pollença**). The walk starts from the car park in front of the **Serra de Tramuntana Information Centre** at **Lluc** monastery.

From the **Serra de Tramuntana Information Centre** (Wp.1 0M), we follow the monastery access road toward the MA-10 then turn left after 150-metres (immediately after the GR turns right) onto a tarmac drive, and then right to go through a stone gateway marked with a red dot. After crossing the football pitch and a wooden bridge at its far left corner, we take the waymarked steps climbing steadily through a chaos of delicately fluted rock.

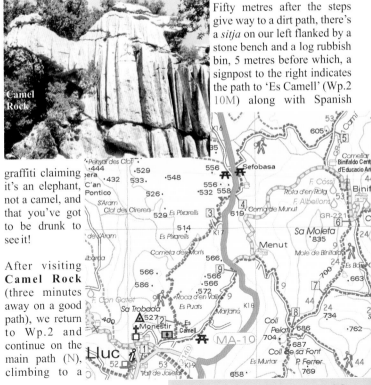

Camel Rock

Fifty metres after the steps give way to a dirt path, there's a *sitja* on our left flanked by a stone bench and a log rubbish bin, 5 metres before which, a signpost to the right indicates the path to 'Es Camell' (Wp.2 10M) along with Spanish graffiti claiming it's an elephant, not a camel, and that you've got to be drunk to see it!

After visiting **Camel Rock** (three minutes away on a good path), we return to Wp.2 and continue on the main path (N), climbing to a level junction of dirt trails, where we turn left for **Es Pixarells**. After crossing a gentle rise, we pass two benches with fine views of the **Puigs Roig** and **Caragoler**, then zigzag into a shallow depression, passing a series of *sitjes* and rocks riddled by erosion. Bearing right then left out of the depression, we climb to the **Es Pixarells Área Recreativa**, where we take the partially concreted track up towards the MA-10. Below the **Área Recreativa** noticeboard and in front of the water point, we take a narrow path through the woods behind the parking bays (Wp.3 40M).

After passing a *sitja* and crossing a small outcrop of rock, we descend on cobbled steps towards a flat, rock fringed glade, formerly a designated camping area, as attested by the stubby posts marking tent placements (camping is forbidden here now). At the bottom of the steps, we turn right on a rough way climbing over rocks to a path leading into a labyrinth of rocks alongside the MA-10. After passing an old red waymarking arrow, we bear left at a waypost and almost immediately find another waypost and a *sitja*. Maintaining direction, we cross two large outcrops of rock, hopefully with cairns on them, to a third tall waypost, where we bear left again on a reasonably clear stretch leading to an apparent dead-end in a small glade. Just to the right of this glade there's an electricity pylon and two cairns marking a way across the rocks to the right of the pylon, after which a clear path back to the road emerges at a gateway directly in front of the principal **Menut Área Recreativa** (Wp.4 50M).

Crossing the road and the **Área Recreativa** car-park, we go behind the main building and the barbecue hut to follow a broad, trodden way descending between picnic tables (NW) to the small parking area at the bottom of the *Área Recreativa*. Bearing right, we take a broad, gated dirt track climbing towards **Puig Tomir**. Ignoring all minor branch tracks, we stay on this track as it meanders through mixed woodland, climbing through a series of concreted sections, eventually passing between two stone pillars to join the **Camí Vell de Pollença** and the **GR221** (Wp.5 95M). Turning right, we follow the **Camí Vell** to the **Binifaldó Education Centre**, the large farmhouse visible for the last few minutes, where we emerge on the road to the **Binifaldó** bottling plant. Turning left, we follow the road up through an S-bend until it bears left through the bottling plant gates (Wp.6 110M), where we climb over the stone/concrete stile next to the closed gates on the right.

Ignoring the dirt track after the stile, we take the narrow path on the right (signposted 'Son Amer/Lluc'), which winds through the woods for fifteen minutes before rejoining the dirt track (Wp.7 125M). Bearing right, we climb to an unnamed, unmarked *coll* and continue on the dirt track down to **Coll Pelat** (Wp.8 135M). The GR continues on the level for **Lluc via Son Amer**, but we turn sharp right on a branch track descending toward the MA-10.

After an easy fifteen minute descent, we cross an immense ladder-stile over a fenced stone wall leading into the public **Menut** farm. Ignoring a branch 50 metres later, we continue straight ahead to go to the left of the farmhouse and rejoin the **Binifaldó** access lane, 250 metres from the MA-10. Turning left on the MA-10, we cross the road 75 metres later, just before the bend, and take a stony track (Wp.9 160M) gently descending between holm oak, olive trees and pine. Ignoring all subsequent branches, we follow this track for a little over fifteen minutes, rejoining the outward route at the wooden bridge behind the football field.

10 MORTITX: L'HAVANOR

A perfect combination of easy walking and wild landscape, the **Havanor** track behind the **Mortitx** estate is very possibly the finest stroll on the island.

Our previous version of this itinerary followed the track right to the end and then a little bit more, and it had been my intention to extend the itinerary for the new edition by trail-blazing an off-path descent to **Rafal d'Ariant** and the bottom of the **Mortitx** gorge. However, readers' reports have suggested that the original access restrictions designed to protect the resident Black Vultures during the breeding season are gradually being extended, prohibiting walkers from passing the **Coll d'es Vent or** even, in one instance, the **Torrent de Comes**.

When we last re-walked the route, there was no evidence of these restrictions (notwithstanding the fact that one reader had actually sent us a photo of the signboard outlining them!); however, we felt it best to limit ourselves to the signposted route to the new **Havanor Refuge**, on the assumption that a public picnic spot will probably remain accessible.

Havanor refuge

The walk is considerably shorter than it was, but no matter. It could become even shorter and still remain a gem. For up-to-date news on when and where you can go, check with the **Tramuntana Information Centre** at **Lluc**.

2	1½ H	6.5 km	⬆150m ⬇150m	out & back	0

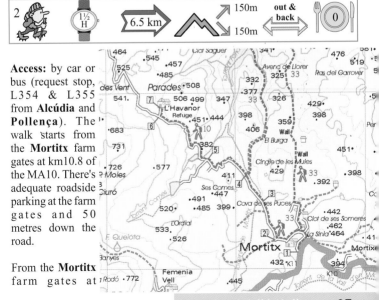

Access: by car or bus (request stop, L354 & L355 from **Alcúdia** and **Pollença**). The walk starts from the **Mortitx** farm gates at km10.8 of the MA10. There's adequate roadside parking at the farm gates and 50 metres down the road.

From the **Mortitx** farm gates at

km10.8 of the MA10 (Wp.1 0M), we follow the driveway track as it passes a tennis court and the main farmhouse, after which it descends to the left, passing the estate winery before reaching a Y-junction at a corner of the principal vineyard (Wp.2 8M), where we fork right for the 'Refugi'.

A little over 400 metres later, at the end of the vineyard, we cross a high ladder stile into the Black Vulture reserve (Wp.3 13M).

We now traverse a classic Mallorcan rockscape dotted with tormented olive, oleaster, and carob trees, the rocks and trees conspiring in their convolutions like weird sisters in an ancient fable. 400 metres into the reserve, we pass a narrow, cairn-flanked turning on the right into the **Mortitx Gorge** (Wp.4), a worthwhile detour if you don't intend doing Walk 33.

After climbing through a concrete bend, we come to a major Y-junction (Wp.5 28M). The track on the left climbs to the upper dam on the **Torrent de Comes**, a ten minute diversion that is also worthwhile, especially if access is restricted further along the **Havanor** track.

the dam wall

For the main walk however, we fork right to cross the lower dam wall and climb along a surfaced track toward a distinctive chimney of rock.

rock 'chimney'

200 metres after the rock chimney, we fork right (Wp.6 40M) to descend to the **Havanor** refuge (Wp.7 43M), which is locked but has a pleasant picnic table, a stoop for shelter, and a chemical toilet tucked around the back. We return by the same route.

overlooking the Mortitx gorge from the Havanor track

The **Bóquer Valley** is a bird watcher's paradise, but most visitors are lured by its unspoiled beauty and a walk that's suitable for all but the most resolutely sedentary holidaymakers. It can be crowded, but it's no less beautiful for that, and if it's solitude you're after, take the extension - nobody's going to be following you up there!

The Bóquer Valley

The mass migration of birds begins in April, but there are notable sightings for 'twitchers' all year round, in particular the rare Audouin Gull, which is found only in the Balearics and Turkey.

*	Short Version 1, Extension 5
**	+ 1h05 for the extension, Short Version 1h-1h15
***	Short Version 80 metres, Extension + 270 metres

Short Version To **Coll del Moro**	**Stroll** To Wp.2, returning via the alternative path.	**Additional stroll** The **Bosquet de Bóquer**, 300 metres from Wp.1 along the **Formentor** road.	**Extension** Cavall Bernat (see text)

Access: on foot from **Port de Pollença**. To reach the start on foot, we follow **Port de Pollença** esplanade (NNE) to the **Restaurante Los Pescadores** and turn left on **Avenguda de Bocchoris**, crossing **Carrer de Formentor** to a pine and tamarisk-flanked promenade, the **Área Pública Bóquer**, **Camí de Bóquer** (Wp.1 0M) (signposted from the new bypass to Formentor if arriving by car).

At the end of the **Camí de Bóquer**, formerly the driveway to the castellated **Bóquer** farm ahead, we cross the road and take the **Predio Bóquer** track up to the farm gates.

Going through the main gates, we pass in front of the house, go through a second gate, and bear right through a third gate (the Mallorcans do love a good gate!), after which we follow the broad path climbing gently between the **Serra del Cavall Bernat** and the **Creveta Ridge**.

Going through a narrow defile formed by two pinnacles of rock, we pass a lime-kiln within sight of a small stand of pine, after which the valley broadens and the outline of the bay becomes clearer. The path crosses a stone wall (Wp.2 20M), just before which a branch track doubles back on the right. Up to our left, we can see one of the 'eyes' through the **Cavall Bernat**. The shallow dip in the ridge to the right of the eye is **La Capellassa**, our objective on the extension. For the present though, we continue towards the sea and, five minutes later, reach a branch path on the left (Wp.3 25M) marked by a large cairn. This is the extension.

If you're not doing the extension
Stay on the main path for another five minutes to the **Coll del Moro**, identifiable by a large pile of stones.

For the short version
Stop at the *coll* and return via the same route or the alternative stroll.

For the full version
Bear right at the *coll* and follow the cairns down the valley along a wide path that reaches the beach fifteen minutes later.

The beach itself isn't up to much, stony, speckled with patches of tar, and strewn with piles of flotsam, but the bay is unspoilt and the water's good for swimming in fine weather, though hazardous in rough seas due to the rocks and debris.

Extension
The scramble up to **La Capellassa** on the **Cavall Bernat** is nigh on indescribable, but if you've got sturdy legs and a hunger for stunning views, it's a must. Turning left at Wp.2, we descend a rough but clear path beside a stone wall, at the end of which we start climbing.

The path becomes increasingly difficult to distinguish from other patches of bare ground, but following the cairns we climb to the right of a smooth outcrop of rock. The cairns are confusing here, so bear in mind you're not going anywhere specific and where you are going is up all the way!

As we near **La Capellassa**, the path clears briefly before disappearing again. In the last 50 metres, various routes splinter off from one another, the main cairn-marked route bearing left toward the **Cavall Bernat** proper. It is possible to follow the ridge all the way to **Cala St. Vicenç**, but this is notoriously difficult and not recommended. Instead, we bear right, straight up a pathless slope aiming for the lowest point on the ridge.

But don't hurry. There's a sheer drop on the far side and it's not one to confront suddenly. If the route up was indescribable, so are the views from the top, taking in the jagged grandeur of **Formentor** to the east and toe-curling cliffs to the west.

A forty minute climb is followed by a twenty-five minute descent along the same route, picking our way from cairn to cairn with extreme caution since it's very unstable underfoot. However, instead of bearing right towards Wp.3, we bear left halfway down to follow goat paths towards the bay, emerging 50 metres north-west of **Coll del Moro** on a minor path, where we bear left for a gentle descent to a boulder-strewn watercourse leading to the beach.

To return, we climb between the remains of old walls 10 metres east of the watercourse. Joining the main cairn-marked path, we wind up the eastern side of the valley, passing ancient terracing walls and an old *canaleta* outlet, reaching the **Coll del Moro** fifteen minutes later.

For a slight variation on the return and for the stroll
Bear left at Wp.2 (5M from **Coll del Moro**) on a broad track climbing slightly towards **Penyal Roig**. The track flattens out and dwindles to a path in front of a concrete hut with a green door, before dropping down below a narrow stone-capped *canaleta* to rejoin the outward route just short of the defile.

Despite its proximity to one of the island's largest beach resorts, the **Alcúdia Peninsula** is a surprisingly wild place, long forsaken by man apart from the aborted **Bon Aire** *urbanización*, a small golf course, and the military installations on **Cap des Pinar**. At first glance, it can seem a bit barren, but once the eyes are used to it, there's a distinct charm to the folds of the land and the rough vegetation.

Unfortunately, the only bus service stops at **Mal Pas** and only runs in summer. Using the extension, this walk gives pedestrian access to the longer tours of the **Talaia d'Alcúdia** and **Penya Roja** (see Walks 35 & 46). It also serves as a lovely introduction to the peninsula and the island's flora, passing through a profusion of nearly all Mallorca's classic shrubs: *pistacia*, euphorbia, *carritx*, asphodel, broom, dwarf palm and more.

All three walks on the **Alcúdia** peninsula have now been sign and wayposted, and the approach roads are dotted with mapboards..

* + 1h if walking from Alcúdia   ** + 6km if walking from Alcúdia

Access: by car and on foot from **Alcúdia**. Motorists take the **Mal Pas** road from **Alcúdia**, turn right at the **Bodega del Sol** bar, and follow the **Camí de la Muntanya** to the end of the tarmac at the entrance of the **Victoria Área Natural**. If you're walking from **Alcúdia**, take the side-road just south of the Repsol Petrol Station and, after 100 metres, bear right on the lane skirting **Sa Vinya**. After another 100 metres, turn left on the **Camí S'Alou**. We then follow this attractive lane for 2 km until it joins the **Camí de la Muntanya**. The start of the walk is 500 metres on our right, where the tarmac ends at the entrance to the **Victoria Área Natural**.

Camí S'Alou

From the entrance gates (Wp.1 0M), we bear left on a broad track (see picture on the next page), climbing through the trees. After a couple of minutes, we pass a path to the right signposted **Coll de na Benet** - our return route, though if you don't have a car and want to climb the **Talaia** (Walk 35) it would be more logical to take this turning now.

Our track climbs gently then dips into a valley as it dwindles to a path with good views of **Pollença** bay. After crossing two watercourses, we climb toward the terraced garden and large greenhouse of an enormous hilltop villa, behind which we have our first sight of the **Talaia**. We then descend alongside the **Bon Aire** *urbanización* amid a mass of shrubbery, passing a branch coming in from the left, after which we gradually bear right (ENE), crossing a

The start of the main walk

small rise, before joining a dirt track above the **Torrent de Fontanelles** (Wp.2 25M).

Bearing right, we cross the torrent just below a tiny dam, where we leave the track and take a signposted path up the torrent's right bank. This pleasant path, occasionally invaded by shrubbery, climbs gently alongside the torrent before crossing back onto the left bank, from where we can see the clump of trees at the **Coll de na Benet**.

Taking a break in the Torrent de Fontanelles

Continuing our climb, we cross the torrent three times, before a final, slightly steeper ascent, brings us to the crossroads at the *coll* (Wp.3 45M). For a slightly longer walk, carry straight on here to follow Walk 35 in reverse to the **Camí de la Muntanya**; for a very long walk, turn left for the **Talaia** (see Walks 35 & 46); otherwise, we turn right.

Climbing steadily, we cross a minor *coll* from where we can see the **Illa d'Alcanada** (S), after which a final brief climb brings us over the **Claper des Gegants** knoll, within sight of **Alcúdia**'s commercial port. The path levels out and descends very slightly to skirt another knoll, after which we gradually zigzag down (as always, much further that one would expect), traversing a fallen pine and head-high euphorbia, and detouring round another fallen pine, almost immediately after which we rejoin our outward route at the 'Coll de na Benet' sign, thirty minutes from the *coll*, and two minutes from our starting point.

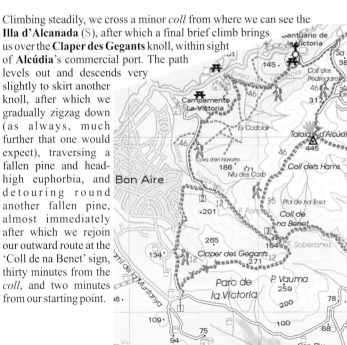

Sa Bruta is the rocky ridge between **Peguera** and the C719 **Túnel de Son Vich**. The path itself is not especially interesting, but the views from the summit of **Es Castellot de na Marío** are superb, taking in the entire coast between **Cap d'es Llamp** and **Magaluf**, the **Garrafa** ridge, the mountains behind **Sant Elm**, and the summits of **S'Esclop** and **Galatzó**. Ideal for the first day if you're based in or around **Peguera**.

*in **Peguera**

Access: on foot from **Peguera**. The walk starts at the western end of **Peguera**, on the northern side of the **Cala Fornells** roundabout, diagonally opposite the **Casa Pepe** supermarket, and begins with a steady climb through the swathe of villas behind **Peguera**.

Setting off on **Carrer de la Talaia** (Wp.1 0M), we take the third turning on the left, **Carrer Dr. Noe** (Wp.2), then fork right fifty metres later on **Carrer Tamarinde**. We then bear right on **Calle Bellavista**, which continues as **Carrer de Baladre**, passing the **Monte Esmeralda** flats, beyond which the road ends in a turning circle (Wp.3 20M).

Continuing on a stony track through the gates of an abandoned *urbanización* project, we climb toward a small stone ruin, forty metres short of which we bear right on a broad trail marked with cairns (Wp.4). Following the cairns, we climb gently to steadily amid scattered, scorched pine, and large bushes of cistus, *pistacia lentiscus* and broom, with fine views over the **Ensenada de Santa Ponça**, passing en route a cairn-marked path on our left (Wp.5 30M) (part of the alternative return route). The trail gradually curves round the mountain, bringing the hinterland into view, after which we turn sharp left, leaving the broad trail and taking a clear path flanked by cairns (Wp.6 35M).

Looking east, before the first rocky outcrop

Fifty metres later, at a junction of paths marked by a large cairn, we bear right (Wp.7; the path directly ahead is also part of the alternative return) and climb steadily to steeply, passing junctions with two more faint paths (SW & NE), shortly after which we come to a large outcrop of rock.

Ignoring a cairn to the right, we can either scramble directly over this outcrop, or skirt round to its left on a rough way strewn with felled trees. In either case, on the far side we recover a clear path and see the craggy summit of **Es**

The final ascent

Castellot de na Marío fifty metres to the north.

The path winds into the base of the rocks before curving into a final easy, but slightly vertiginous (slightly more so in descent!) ledge leading to the top (Wp.8 40M), from where we have superb views through 360°.

The return is generally done by the same route, but if you wish to extend the walk a little, there are two alternative paths. Whatever you do though, take care on the ledge descent, especially when it's wet.

Alternative returns

The first alternative begins at the junction of paths marked with a large cairn (Wp.7). The path to the south west follows a contour line before curving back to rejoin our outward route thirty metres above Wp.5.

The path to the south-west from Wp.5 also loops through the woods before joining a logging track (Wp.9 60M) fifty metres behind the stone ruin seen earlier. From here we can either turn left to recover our outward route or turn right and follow the track, which immediately dwindles to a broad trail, descending through the woods to the southwest.

This trail eventually emerges on the wide and, at this point, virtually unused **Carrer Bonavida** (Wp.10 75M) behind the brick red, pale pink and beige apartments (not nearly so appalling as they sound!) of **Hotel Don Antonio**.

Turning left, we follow the road behind the apartments and down past the hotel. When **Carrer Bonavida** swings right at the **Complejo Residencial La Colina** (Wp.11), we carry straight on, following **Carrer del Bosc** until it curves into **Carrer Llimonara** (Wp.12). Bearing right shortly after the 'zona verde' signs (Wp.13), we return to the centre of **Peguera** via **Carrer de l'Olivera**.

14 PUIGPUNYENT: THE CAMÍ VELL DE ESTELLENCS

Many of the old Royal Ways of Spain have been obliterated by dirt tracks and new roads, and if there's one thing Mallorca doesn't lack, it's twisting, turning, spiralling, dizzying switchback roads. Yet despite the fact that it's the most direct route between **Puigpunyent** and **Estellencs**, nobody seems to have thought that it would be a good idea to asphalt the **Camí Real** or **Camí Vell d'Estellencs**, for which we can be grateful, since the oversight has preserved some very agreeable walking country. In this itinerary, we follow the old royal way and charcoal burners' tracks to explore the lovely, peaceful countryside above **Son Fortesa**, one of the most impressive manor houses in the area.

3 | 2½H | 9.9 km | 375m / 375m | 2* in **Puigpunyent**

*in **Puigpunyent**

Access: on foot from **Puigpunyent**. Our itinerary starts at kilometre 1 of the MA-1101. To reach the start from the 'Cantonada Escola' bus-stop in the centre of **Puigpunyent**, head uphill, past **Restaurant ses Cotxeries**, bearing left after 600 metres on the **Carretera Nova d'Estellencs**. The kilometre post is at a Y-junction 200 metres later (Wp.1 0M).

While the MA-1101 swings right behind the km1 marker, we fork left and carry straight on through the gate 75 metres later, where there are signs prohibiting cars, motorbikes and cyclists. We follow this lane, which is particularly lovely in spring, toward the peak of **Galatzó** poking over the treetops. After a little over a kilometre, the lane climbs alongside the high, eastern wall of the **Son Fortesa** manor house, then swings left to approach the house from the northeast, at which point a waypost marks two tracks off to our right (Wp.2 14M).

the Son Fortesa lane

The clearer track with black gates goes through the **Son Fortesa** farmyard, but we take the nearer and narrower of the two tracks, which has a rusty gate and a sign for the 'Camí Vell d'Estellencs'. After going through a bedstead gate, we rejoin the main track (Wp.3 23M) and turn right, beginning our steady climb.

When the track veers sharp right beside a large boulder that has broken away from the embankment, we carry straight on, following a wayposted shortcut (Wp.4 31M) that rejoins the main track 100 metres later, within sight of the abandoned **Sa Muntanya** farmhouse - worth crossing the track here to check out the small ruin off to our right, which has been pieced together (it does rather resemble a jigsaw puzzle) with stone and some wonderful homemade bricks.

home-made bricks

We continue along the track, climbing gently past a small spring below the old farmhouse, to the northeast of which the track swings sharp left to a junction, where we bear right, staying on the main track as it enters the woods that are such a feature of the Tramuntana (Wp.5 41M). Forking left at the next Y-junction (Wp.6 45M), we climb steadily on a narrow track that eventually goes through a gateway in a wall, 20 metres after which, when the track doubles back to the left, we carry straight on along a broad walking trail (Wp.7 49M).

The steady climb continues, occasionally on sections of

the Sa Muntanyas spring

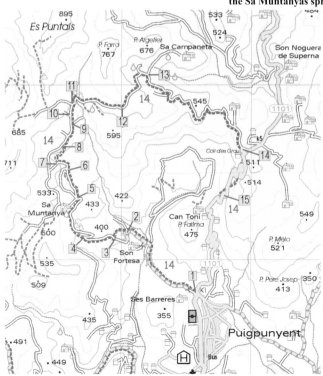

cobbling, but mainly on a carpet of Holm oak leaf mulch, crossing another track then rejoining it 50 metres later (Wp.8 54M). Bearing right, we climb to an intersection with the bend of another track (Wp.9 58M), at which point we carry straight on (the left hand branch), still climbing and ignoring an overgrown branch off to the left 75 metres later (Wp.10).

Eventually, we come to a signposted T-junction where we turn right for 'Es Grau' (Wp.11 62M). Passing a branch on the left and a large lime-kiln on our right, we follow the main track, forking left at a wayposted junction after a sitja and small ruin, after which the track gradually dwindles to a trail.

At a point where two walls converge, we bear left through a gateway (Wp.12 77M), and descend across terraces in an easterly direction. At a junction with a narrow dirt track, we turn right then right again 50 metres later (Wp.13 87M). We now simply follow this track through a series of gates (either open or unlocked) all the way to the **Coll d'es Grau** (Wp.14 112M) and the main road between **Puigpunyent** and **Esporles**.

Perhaps 'main' road is a slight exaggeration. First of all, it's the only road, second; it's rarely more than three strides wide, and thirdly, it twists back and forth like an agitated snake, making it better suited for bicycles than cars, all of which is to the good, since this is our route back to **Puigpunyent**.

Galatzó and S'Esclop seen from Es Puntals

Turning right, we cross the coll and take the first of three wayposted shortcuts that eventually emerge just short of the km3.1 kilometre-post (Wp.15 122M), after which we follow the road for the last two kilometres back to the start.

15 SON MARROIG: SA FORADADA

In 1867, the Archduke Ludwig Salvador, a lowly member of the Austrian royal family, settled in Mallorca and set about turning himself into a one man preservation society, buying up landed estates like the things were going out of fashion and laying the fabulous bridleway on the **Teix** massif (see Walks 40 & 49). Among his properties was **Son Marroig**, the starting point for this classic stroll down to **Sa Foradada**, the spectacular 'pierced' headland between **Valldemossa** and **Deià**.

Some books say you need to ask permission to do the walk (confirmed by notices at the start), others that permission is implicit in purchasing a ticket to visit the house. We bought no ticket, couldn't find anyone interested in giving us permission, and the bar-keeper said we didn't need it.

Access: by car or bus (L210 between **Palma**, **Valldemossa**, **Deià** and **Sóller**). The **Son Marroig** car park is at km 65.5 of the MA-10.

From the main doors of **Son Marroig** (Wp.1 0M), we walk up the tarmac lane (SE) past the lion-head fountain and, 50 metres later, climb over the ladder-stile at the green '*No-pasa-sin autorizacion*' gate.

Following the initially concreted track on the other side of the gate, we bear right at the Y-junction a couple of hundred metres later.

The stony track winds down past superb cliffs that look like they're melting before it is joined by a dirt track (Wp.2 35M).

Sa Foradada, as seen from Walk 49

After strolling along to the neck of the peninsula (Wp.3 45M), we have a choice between a swim from the **Playola** jetty, a drink in the bar (rarely open before midday), or (not recommended since only climbers can descend to the hole) a scramble onto the **Foradada** rock itself. We return by the same route (85M).

An attractive short walk on cobbled trails and dirt tracks visiting the **Mirador de ses Barques** and the head of the ever popular **Balitx Valley**.

Access: by car or on foot (add 80M return) from **Port de Sóller** via the MA2124. There's parking for two small cars on the northern side of the coll.

From **Coll d'en Marques** (Wp.1 0M), just as the road starts to descend toward **Sóller**, we take the tarmac lane on the left, bearing right 30 metres from the road on an unmarked cobbled trail. After going through a first gate, we climb steeply to a second gate, beyond which we continue climbing until the trail bears right and we join a dirt track.

Bearing left, we climb towards a new house, just before which we turn right onto a cairn-marked path. 50 metres along this path, we go through a gate under the natural arch of a carob tree, beyond which we walk between crumbling retaining walls, initially on the level, then climbing slightly to a point where a steel cable has been set in the rocks as a handrail. 30 metres later, we join a dirt track beside a small concrete cabin. Maintaining direction (SE), we follow the track behind the cabin, going through two green gates, the second next to an old farmhouse.

The track then descends through a concreted bend before winding along the contour line to a second concreted bend (Wp.2 25M), where we turn left on a broad cobbled path. At the second of two large metal gates, we ignore a branch to the right and maintain direction (N) to join a dirt track (Wp.3 35M). Bearing left for a few metres, we recover the path, which climbs via a cobbled stretch to intersect with Walk 42 at Wp.3 (Wp.4 45M).

Crossing the **Balitx** track, we take the signposted path (the **Camí Vell de Balitx**) for the 'Mirador de ses Barques'.

After crossing a small rise, we bear right on a wayposted trail descending to the *mirador* (Wp.5 55M).

Cami Vell de Balitx

On the far side of the mirador car park, we take the 'Fornalutx, Port Sóller' path, which descends to a signposted junction of routes for 'Fornalutx' and 'Sóller'.

Opting for the **Sóller** path, we descend steadily through a lovely natural tunnel formed by a deeply embedded cobbled path and a high canopy of oak trees. Joining a stony track, we bear left (Wp.6 65M), passing a gate topped with metal letters spelling out 'Es Figueral', 100 metres after which, we leave the track (Wp.7 70M), taking a waymarked path below the house on the left.

When the path emerges on a dirt track, we turn left then immediately right to join a concrete track, 10 metres along which a signpost indicates 'Port Sóller' to the right. After passing the entrance to **Ses Moncades**, the concrete deteriorates and eventually gives way to dirt. The track winds along the contour before climbing slightly to a sharp right hand bend where it is concreted again. Ignoring the waymarked path on the left, we stay on the track as it climbs to rejoin our outward route at Wp.2 (85M).

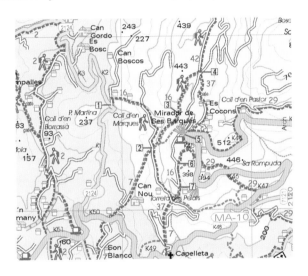

This variation on the classic climb from **Sóller** to **Can Prohom** is an ideal introduction to walking in Mallorca. Following country lanes, cobbled donkey trails, dirt tracks and clear paths, it's easy walking all the way, winding between typically well-maintained terraces dotted with modest cabins and the occasional magisterial country home. Frequent shady passages mean this is a practical itinerary on a hot day, and a dense fringe of wild gladioli will reward flower-lovers in spring.

3   2-2¼ H   *   9.5 km   350m / 350m   1

* + 20 minutes return to **Can Prohom**

Extension	**Stroll**
Turn left at Wp.10. Follow the dirt track for 50 metres then take the broad path skirting the field, arriving at the chapel just below **Can Prohom** (10M from Wp.10).	Take the bus to **Can Prohom** for the descent back to **Sóller**
	Short Versions
	See text

Access: on foot from **Sóller**. The walk starts from **Plaza d'Espanya**, where the tourism office is.

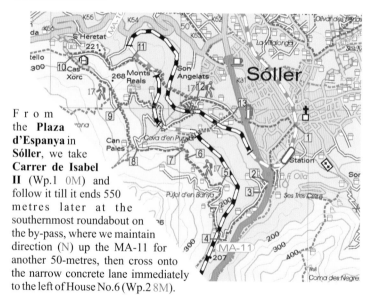

From the **Plaza d'Espanya** in **Sóller**, we take **Carrer de Isabel II** (Wp.1 0M) and follow it till it ends 550 metres later at the southernmost roundabout on the by-pass, where we maintain direction (N) up the MA-11 for another 50-metres, then cross onto the narrow concrete lane immediately to the left of House No.6 (Wp.2 8M).

Forking left twice in the first 100 metres, we climb steeply, carrying straight on (the right hand branch) when we run into a U-bend (Wp.3 13M), after which the gradient eases off. We soon put the racket of the by-pass behind us as the lane winds through immaculately maintained terraces of olive and carob trees. Veering right at a junction with a cobbled trail (Wp.4 31M), we stay on the lane to cross the **Palma-Sóller** railway line 100 metres later. The dwindling end of the surfaced lane curves away to the left in front of a house with a large, arched gate and a weather-beaten sign on the wall for 'Camino de Casteo por s'Heretat y Can Prohom', at which point we carry straight on along a dirt track (Wp.5 38M), that becomes a path a little under 300 metres later. A lovely, shady stroll below overhanging oak leads to a triple fork, where we ignore the gated branches on the left and descend to the right (Wp.6 48M) to the signposted junction with the **Camí de Rocafort** (Wp.7 51M) where we turn right for a shorter walk or carry straight on for the main walk, soon reaching a stretch where the old *camí* has been widened to a dirt track. After a gentle descent, we climb behind a recently restored house, where we find a stretch of concrete and a waypost indicating we leave the track to recover the original narrow path (Wp.8 56M).

The path climbs steps crossing the **Cinc Ponts Torrent**, beyond which we cross a wayposted junction of dirt tracks. Maintaining direction (NW), we climb steeply on a rough concrete track, recovering the path 30 metres later at another waypost and painted rock sign in front of **Can Paies**. The path tunnels through a dense overgrowth of pistacia then continues through successive stretches of shade and sun, level and descent, before going through a rough wire gate. Strolling along immaculate terraces, we approach a large house fronted by a tall palm tree, just before which we come to our second shortcut option, a signposted path on the right, **Camí des Monts Reals** (Wp.9 66M).

To continue on the **Camí de Castello**, we go through the gated courtyard behind the large house, taking care to shut both gates behind us, after which a steady climb along a cobbled donkey trail brings us through another rough gate onto a dirt track between a small cabin and a stand of pine on a knoll topped with a gazebo.

We bear right on the dirt track to maintain direction (NW), already in sight of

La Muleta. The track becomes a tarmac lane passing behind the luxurious **Cas Xorc Hotel**, at the gates of which (Wp.10 81M) we have a choice, turning left to continue along the **Camí de Castello** to **Can Prohom** or right to descend to **Sóller**.

Turning right for **Sóller**, we follow the wayposted dirt track, the **Camí des Rost**, past a first branch on the left

Can Prohom

(ending in a pleasant picnic spot if desired). The track then climbs towards a gate, just before which we bear left on a wayposted path (Wp.11 91M). After going through a rough gate, we join a cobbled path that soon broadens to a stepped donkey trail. Following a 100 metre stretch thinly coated with tarmac, we recover the cobbled trail which descends steeply to the junction with the **Camí des Monts Real** (see Wp.12). The cobbles eventually run into a tarmac lane, passing the junction for **Camí de Rocafort** (Wp.13), 50 metres after which we bear left at House Nº1 to rejoin the **Sóller** by-pass in front of the petrol station (115M). For the town centre, take the lane to the right of the petrol station.

18 CÚBER: L'OFRE

L'Ofre is the distinctive conical peak southeast of **Sóller** that, from a distance, appears to be mantled in a dense cloak of trees except for a small tonsure on top. Though not particularly high, it's such a distinctive summit that its ascent has become something of a classic and it can get a little crowded at times, but one shouldn't be too sniffy about things that are popular, since they're often popular for a reason.

L'Offre and Es Cornadors from Sóller

In this instance, that tonsure really is a spectacular little eyrie, offering fabulous views of the more dramatic summits to the west ringing the **Ofre** farm. Get there early, though, otherwise it's elbow room only.

3   23/4 H   10.8 km   300m / 300m   out & back   0

Access: by car and bus. Our itinerary starts at the **Cúber** parking area/bus stop at km34 of the MA10. If arriving by the L354 bus (seasonal service), asked to be dropped off at **Cúber**.

Stroll

A simple tour round the reservoir is very pleasant when the weather is too hot or too wild to contemplate anything more arduous.

Ofre seen from the reservoir

From the **Cúber** parking area (Wp.1 0M), we contour round the reservoir, either via the GR on its northern side, or the tarmac lane/dirt track on the southern shore. At the far end of the lake, we go through the gates into the **Ofre** estate (Wp.2 28M) from where we can see the cone-like summit of the same name.

1200 metres later, in front of the uninhabited **Binimorat** farmhouse, the GR forks right, leaving the main dirt track (Wp.3 34M) to follow a broad, intermittently cobbled trail that climbs gently to the **Coll de l'Ofre** (Wp.4 45M), where there's a tall metal crucifix planted in a pile of stones and fine views open out toward the summits surrounding the **Ofre** farmhouse.

Turning left, initially off-path, we head for a black and white hunting rectangle and a red '*Camino Particular Prohibido el Paso*' sign (don't worry, this really is a classic, everybody ignores the sign!), behind which a rough track winds through a bend before climbing in an easterly direction.

The track eventually levels out within sight of **Coll d'es Cards** (up to our right) before emerging in an open flat grassy area directly below the coll. On the far side of the flat grassy area, we intersect with Walk 30 at an inverted Y-junction (Wp.5 55M). Turning right, we climb to the **Coll d'es Cards** (Wp.6 58M). Bearing right, we cross the rocks to the left of a metal pylon, behind which cairns mark a rough trail pieced together from patches of sheep paths. Keeping an eye out for the cairns, we climb steadily (SW) to a junction with the southern approach (Wp.7 70M) just below the summit, which is reached by following the red and blue waymarks up to the right.

The descent is made by the southerly path, which skitters down quite steeply at first. Following the clearer traces wherever the path appears to splinter, we eventually reach level ground and a cairnmarked Y-junction on the edge of a stand of mature pine (Wp.8 84M).

Taking the fork to the right, we descend alongside a wall to join a broad dirt track at the **Coll d'en Poma** (Wp.9 87M).

Coll de l'Ofre

A faint way directly in front of us marks the start of the descent to **Pas de na Maria** and is worth taking for a few metres to see the dilapidated remains of a hugely improbable sightseers' telescope. Sight-seen, we take the dirt track to the northwest, enjoying an agreeable stroll through the woods before rejoining the main **Ofre** track just below the **Coll de l'Ofre** (Wp.4 101M).

To return to the starting point we simply retrace our steps to the reservoir, then follow the opposite shoreline to the one taken earlier.

Famously constructed by a Mallorcan pig farmer after the great engineers of the age said it wasn't possible, the **Canaleta de Massanella** is an eighteenth century *aquifer* that is still in use today, bringing water down from the **Font des Prat** to **Mancor del Valle**. The fact that the professionals baulked at building in such inhospitable terrain may explain why the canaleta has often been regarded as altogether too hairy by many walkers, myself not excluded, who fear they'll end up on all fours, peering over the precipice, wondering whether stamp collecting wouldn't be a wiser pastime.

In fact, the dangers are often exaggerated. They are real and should not be dismissed out of hand, but it's a lot less vertiginous than many aquifers I've walked (or, in one instance, crawled) and described in other publications, and so long as you have a reasonable head for heights and are careful where you put your feet, the risk is not great. The rewards, however, in terms of isolation, views, and the sheer thrill of it all cannot be exaggerated, and even those who don't want to venture onto the *canaleta* should take the time to do the short version, which is a delight in itself. Given the nature of the walk, it is not recommended when the *canaleta* is wet.

Though adequate, GPS reception is not consistent either in the woods or in the lee of the cliffs.

Short Version: to Wp.7 then down onto the bridge to loop back to Wp.4.
Extension: **Mancor del Valle** (see text)

Access: by bus or car. The walk starts from the **Font des Noguer Área Recreativa** just east of km34 of the MA10. If arriving by the L354 bus (seasonal service), asked to be dropped off at **Cúber**, which is 150 metres west of Wp.1

From the **Área Recreativa** (Wp.1 0M) we follow the GR221 signposted 'Font d'es Prat, Refugi des Tossals Verds' alongside a modern concrete *canaleta*, enjoying fine views over **Gorg Blau** and passing three concrete ramps bridging the aquifer. After nearly two and a half kilometres, we cross the aquifer via the fourth ramp (Wp.2 32M).

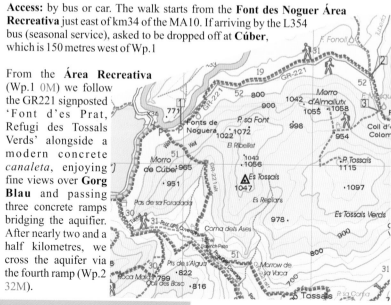

Still following the GR, we climb via a partially cobbled trail to the **Coll d'es Coloms** (Wp.3 39M). 300 metres later, after a gentle descent, we turn left for 'Font d'es Prat' (Wp.4 47M). Ignoring a fork on the left 50 metres later (Wp.5), we stay on the GR until it reaches a signposted junction immediately south of **Font d'es Prat**, where we can already see the partially interred head of the old *canaleta* (Wp.6 53M).

an 'easy' stretch

We leave the GR at this juncture, crossing the small stone bridge immediately after the signpost and bearing right to follow a faint trodden way parallel to the stream. After passing a large limekiln 100 metres later, the path becomes clearer, winding through lovely woodland before joining the *canaleta* proper at two metal hatches (Wp.7 57M).

at the tunnel

Easy strolling continues as the *canaleta* passes above a wooden footbridge (an alternative approach and the turning point for the Short Version), but we soon cross a wall, after which we reach the first vertiginous bit, a delicately arched aqueduct, a little under a metre wide, where you may find yourself (I know I did) proceeding with the concentrated determination of a two year old who is still a little unsteady on his feet.

Thereafter, things get easier again, a rough, rocky slope dotted with trees slanting away below us as we pass a *sitja*, from where we can see a short tunnel on the far side of the valley where the *canaleta* pierces an outcrop of rock.

After the first of several taps set into the wall, the *canaleta* swings right, passing an off-path cairn-marked descent to the right (Wp.8 76M), 130 metres after which, we go through the tunnel - again, slightly vertiginous as we have to step out onto a ledge over a ten metre drop.

At the next bend, wonderful views open out to the south and the drop gets appreciably greater as the *canaleta* starts to descend slightly, passing a fifteen metre stretch which was the only place where I developed a 'Let's hug!' affinity for the rockface.

We then pass above a lovely *sitja* (Wp.9 88M), which is ideal for a picnic spot and where I recommend most people stop unless you want to enjoy some fine views of **Puig de Massanella** (Walk 45) and **Puig n'Ali** or intend doing the extension.

a 'less easy' stretch

Shortly after the picnic *sitja*, the trees close in around us and the *canaleta* descends in a straight line through the woods to a very slight right hand bend where large cairns mark a path descending to the left (Wp.10 93M).

In the unlikely event that you can arrange to be dropped off at the top and picked up at the bottom, this would be a pleasant extension. The path on the left zigzags down through the woods to reach an attractive *casa forestal* half an hour later. Simply bear right and follow the dirt track down the valley to reach the **Son Catlar** restaurant on the **Mancor-Caimari** road in another half hour.

Those of you who don't have the luxury of a lift at the end of the walk but who want to see some fine views of **Massanella** and the surrounding summits can continue along the *canaleta* for another 600 metres as it descends ever more steeply through the woods (you'll have to duck under overhanging branches and skirt two stretches where low branches and fallen trees block the path) until it curves below cliffs to cross a wall, where it gets even steeper and eventually dangerous (Wp.11 108M).

We return via the same route, with the option of forking left 100 metres after the wall north of the aqueduct (Wp.12 166M) to cross the **Torrent des Prat** by the wooden bridge seen earlier, beyond which a clear trail feeds into the GR and brings us back to Wp.4 (172M).

A tiny but testing little itinerary visiting a quite exceptional viewing point at the Martello tower, chapel and customs hut on the **Mola de Tuent**, the headland separating **Cala Tuent** from **Sa Calobra**.

Access: by car - the walk starts from the car park of the **Sant Llorenç** chapel on the **Cala Tuent** branch of the MA2141.

Behind the house attached to the chapel (Wp.1 0M) we take a gravelly path, climbing steeply to the small cliffs north of the *coll*. Shortly before the wall at the top of these cliffs, we pass a vertiginous stretch where a steel cable is set in the rock (well-set at the time of writing, but test it before trusting your weight to it). N.B. If you find this passage

La Mola

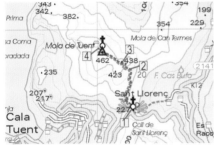

at the limit of the tolerable on the way up, don't insist and simply turn back, as it's more alarming in descent. If you do insist and find yourselves in difficulty on the way back, descend with your back to the drop, which is a lot less hypnotic when you're not looking at it!

Beyond the wall above this cable we come onto a cistus-covered slope from where we already have fine views back towards **Puig Major**. Winding through dense cistus interspersed with the odd clump of *carritx* and *pistacia*, we climb steadily (NNE) on a faint, occasionally slightly confusing path. The path seems to end in a patch of barer ground just below the second outcrop of rocks (Wp.2 20M), but orienting ourselves by a small retaining wall, we maintain our general direction (N) winding through the cistus. Bearing left (SW) at a second cairn then right (NW) 50 metres later, we climb through waist high cistus, thyme, *carritx* and *pistacia* before emerging within sight of the **La Mola** buildings (Wp.3 25M). The path remains crazily overgrown and from a distance is invisible, but heading for the *torre*, the way clarifies itself as we progress. Passing just left of twin pines and ignoring the apparently clearer way through the *carritx* patch on our left, we continue wading through cistus (now chest deep), finally climbing up between the chapel and customs hut, thirty metres west of the tower (Wp.4 35M). The views are stunning, but even more stunning is the quality of the restoration work in this inaccessible site. The buildings are locked, but benches and a few grassy patches in the shade of trees make ideal picnic spots. Return by the same route.

Easy walking along a lovely corniche path to the superbly situated house at **Sa Costera**, with an optional excursion to the **Fábrica de Luz** hydro-electric generating station.

Traditionally part of the **Ses Barques/Sa Calobra** route on which we have the novelty of a return by boat (see Walks 37 & 42 for details).

Cala Tuent

* +35M for the extension and at least an hour for exploring and picnicking
** +150 metres for the extension
*** in **Cala Tuent**

Short Version	**Stroll**	**Extension**
To La Fábrica and back (see text)	(a) bear right at Wp. 2 on the **Tuent/Es Vergeret** path back to the restaurant. (b) to the **Coll de ne Pollo**.	**La Fábrica** (see text).

Access: by car; take the **Cala Tuent** branch off the MA214 then follow the signs for the restaurant. The walk starts on a dirt track in front of the restaurant.

We start from the **Cala Tuent Es Vergeret Bar/Restaurante** on a dirt track between **C'an Boy** and the restaurant gates, signposted 'Sa Costera, Fornalutx, Sóller' (Wp.1 0M).

After 100 metres, we pass a branch track and turn right on a signposted partially cobbled path. Climbing through the woods, we come to a third signpost (Wp.2 7M) below a broad dirt track, which we follow till it ends 75 metres later.

Recovering the cobbled trail, we climb to another dirt track in front of a large, tastefully restored farmhouse, where we turn right. When the track bears left 50 metres later, we take the wayposted path on the right (Wp.3 12M). After a short level stretch, the path climbs gently through mixed woodland, crossing a glade glazed with pine needles and going through a gap in a wall onto the **Coll de ne Pollo**, where views along the coast open out. **Sa Costera** is the house below the wood on the distant headland.

The path descends below a high, dry water chute before climbing to pass the first of two gateways with stone hinge brackets. After the second gateway, a clear green field and large reservoir behind **La Fábrica** are visible down to

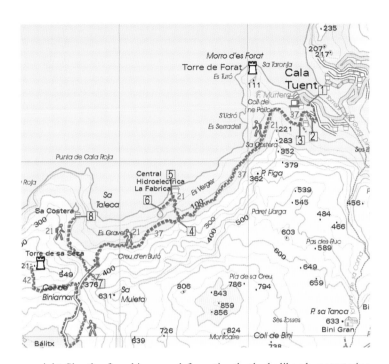

our right. Shortly after a bizarre rock formation that looks like a huge teetering cairn, we come to the signposted path down to 'La Fábrica/Font des Verger' (Wp.4 50M).

Extension / Short Version

Descending 150 metres only to climb right back up again is never a very engaging proposition, but I strongly recommend this extension. Taking the green-arrowed path to the right, we descend steeply, soon coming into view of the far end of the reservoir. After crossing a rickety bridge over the reservoir conduit, we bear right, passing a couple of fig trees, and descend to the idyllically situated and beautifully restored generating station (Wp.5 15M from Wp.4). If you want to swim, the steps down to the turbines in front of the main buildings also lead to a tunnel onto what was once a jetty, just to the right of which a rope helps us descend onto the rocks. Turning left at the rickety bridge leads to the spring feeding the conduit (Wp.6). We return by the same route (20M).

To continue to Sa Costera

We follow the main path (W) along long level stretches interrupted by brief and sometimes not so brief climbs. After a clearing on our right, the path widens to a track and we continue climbing for a little over five minutes before taking a waypoisted shortcut to the right (Wp.7 80M [not counting the extension]). Thirty metres later, we turn right at another waypost and leave the main trail. Descending along a *carritx* lined path, we bear left at a Y-junction and go through a gap in a wall, after which we follow a terrace to **Sa Costera** (Wp.8 100M). Our return by the same route takes one hour and twenty minutes.

An attractive tour along mostly shady paths and tracks through the lovely, well-managed forest of **Bunyola**. If you're after solitude, best avoided on a Sunday. If, on the other hand, you care to witness the glorious spectacle of Spanish families enjoying themselves at their gregarious best (just count the generations), Sunday at the **Cas Garriguer Área Recreativa** is a must. To drive or cycle to **Cas Garriguer**, turn left off the MA-2020 just before the playground and follow **Carrer del Garrigó**, signposted 'Sa Comuna'.

* Short Version (a) & (b) each loop 1½ h (c) 1h return . ** in **Bunyola**

Short Versions	Strolls
(a) turn right after Wp.4 to descend via **Comellar d'en Cupí**	**(a)** from Wp.2 continue down the lane back into **Bunyola**
(b) drive to **Cas Garriguer Área Recreativa** then walk back to Wp.6 to join the main walk	**(b)** in almost any direction from the **Área Recreativa**
(c) as per Stroll 'c' but continue to **Cas Garriguer**	**(c)** drive along the MA-2020 past the cemetery. Turn left at the electricity substation, signposted 'Es Cocons', then carry straight on when the main lane bears left (Wp.10). Park on the flat open area (probably with a pile of rubbish in the middle) after **Can Co** and walk up to the troglodytic dwelling.

Access: on foot from **Bunyola**. The walk starts from the church in the centre of town. There is plenty of roadside parking on the main road through town, the MA2020

From **Bunyola** church (Wp.1 0M), we take **Carrer Mare de Deú de la Neu** past the post office to cross **Calle de Santa Catalina Tomás** and climb the stairway street, **Carrer de la Lluna**. Turning right at the top, we follow **Carrer d'Orient**, ignoring a first stairway to a private house before turning left onto another stairway street, **Carreró de la Comuna**, signposted 'Sa Comuna/Camí des Grau'. Circling the **Villa Teresa**, we climb to a dirt lane leading towards the mottled bluffs of **El Castellet**. When the lane dips down after 100 metres, we turn left on the **Camí d'es Grau** (Wp.2 10M).

Our path climbs steadily (NE) through the woods to the left of the bluffs, passing the first of the red dots that partially waymark our route. Ignoring all branches, we pass a restored lime-kiln, *sitja* and *aljub* before reaching a Y-junction (Wp.3 25M) where we bear right. After levelling off briefly the **Camí des Grau** continues climbing, zigzagging up to a less well defined stretch winding through the pine. A pleasant meander through the woods brings us to a junction with a broader trail signposted 'Mirador/Camí des Grau' (Wp.4 40M). *Mirador* is a big word for a small clearing on the cliffs with a fallen tree for a bench, but it's only 40 metres to our left, and the views <u>are</u> good. Continuing on the broad trail, we cross a slight rise before joining a dirt track (signed 'Bunyola/Comellar d'en Cupí'), on which we continue climbing through a shallow gully shrouded by a canopy of trees to a major junction of dirt tracks (Wp.5 55M). Turning right, we pass a green fire-fighting reservoir,

50 metres after which we join the main track to **Cas Garriguer** (Wp.6 60M). Ignoring the main track, we immediately bear left on a broad, gated branch track.

The track climbs steadily before levelling out then climbing again. Toward the end of a second long level stretch, we turn left onto a clear path marked by a cairn and signpost (Wp.7 85M). A steady climb of a little under ten minutes brings us to the white rock of the *penyal* and a small green hut that looks alarmingly like an ice-cream kiosk, but is presumably a weather station (Wp.8 95M). After enjoying the spectacular view, we retrace our steps to Wp.7.

Opposite the path to the *penyal*, another path, almost invisible from the track but marked by a small cairn, descends steadily then steeply before widening and levelling out for a gentle stroll to the last bend in the main track (Wp.9 115M) above the **Cas Garriguer Área Recreativa**. Descending to the turning circle in front of the forest warden's hut (there's also a public refuge - the key is available from **Bunyola** town hall), we maintain direction (SSW) on a broad trail passing picnic tables and barbecues. We follow this trail and the lane it leads into all the way back to **Bunyola**, passing through perhaps the most attractive woodland landscape on the entire island. You don't want to be reading a book while you're wandering through this exquisite wood, so in brief: after thirty minutes the track goes through a green wooden gate and continues between walled olive groves; five minutes later we pass a troglodytic house; just after the **Villa Maria**, we join a lane (Wp.10 180M).

Ten minutes on this lane brings us to the MA-2020 behind the electricity substation, where we bear right for a fifteen minute walk along the road back to **Bunyola**.

Bunyola woods

23 ORIENT: CASTELL D'ALARÓ

Castell d'Alaró is a <u>very</u> popular walking destination and is best avoided at weekends. Even during the week it's as well to leave early to get there before the guided hiking parties. Most people climb from **Alaró**, but if you have a car, the **Orient** route, on a pleasant, frequently shady path, is far more attractive. Even taking the waymarked shortcuts, the southern approach involves a good three kilometres of wearying tarmac and concrete. The only advantage, apart from public transport, is a more dramatic perspective on the cliffs that made the castle nigh on impregnable (it withstood a siege for two years). The extension, virtually pathless and almost indescribable, is only recommended for those navigating with a GPS 'GoTo' function or the fortunate few possessed of supernatural pathfinding skills.

* + 1h for the extension, Short Version 50M
** + 100 metres for the extension
*** The sanctuary can serve 40 and sleep 17, but book if you want to stay or, on weekends, even eat (Tel: 971 182112 / 971 940503). The bar's open from 9am-11pm, the kitchen from 12am-4pm & 7-10pm.

	Short Version
Extension see text	Drive to Wp.2 and start from there. Turn west just south of km18 on the MA-2100 then first right and follow the tarmac/concrete lane past **Es Verger** (km 4.5) to **Es Pouet** (km 7) where it ends: note, after the restaurant the track gets even narrower!

Access: by car and bus. The walk starts just after km 11.8 of the MA-2100, 150 metres east of the **Hermitage Hotel**. You can usually park at the hotel, but ask permission first. Otherwise, there is a car park in **Orient** village, adding a couple of kilometres of road walking to the itinerary. There is a taxibus service to **Orient** from **Bunyola** (which can be reached by train and bus) bookable a day in advance on 617 365 365. This would also involve the extra kilometres of road walking.

Just after km 11.8 of the MA-2100, 150 metres east of the **Hermitage Hotel**, we take a track climbing into olive groves via a waymarked gate with two signs prohibiting dogs (Wp.1 0M). The broad, chalky white track climbs gently (NE) before narrowing to a well trodden path running along the edge of a terrace. The climb gradually steepens and the path bears right into a shady oak wood. The gradient eases slightly as the oak are interspersed with pine, before a final steady climb brings us onto a track (Wp.2 35M) at the bottom of the gently shelving clearing of **Es Pouet**.

At the top of the clearing, we bear left at the 'Alaró/Santuari y Postat Hostatgeria del Castell d'Alaró'signpost onto long, shallow steps leading to a partially cobbled trail. At the junction with the old path from **Alaró** (Wp.3 50M), we bear left and follow the remaining steps up to the castle gates.

After exploring (cautiously!) the battlements along the west of the ridge, we follow the stone trail (E) up to the sanctuary (Wp.4 60M). Taking the partially ramped steps to the right of the chapel and climbing to the aerial, we can see (E) **Alaró**'s twin peak, **s'Alcaldena**.

Extension

The path to the **Cova de San Antoni** is so obscure it barely exists, but even those wholly lacking a sense of direction can enjoy wandering round the woods to the east, visiting the lime-kilns and *aljibes*. For the more adventurous, cairns mark the way down to the cave, which can be explored, but only with the utmost care and NOT when it's wet.

The onward 'path' begins at the end of the sanctuary terrace, beyond the rough wooden gate where the donkeys are corralled.

GPS users turn to their 'GoTo' function here, but be careful: there's no such thing as a straight line through these woods and you still need to follow the cairns carefully. After Wp.6, if you haven't seen a cairn in the preceding 30 metres, go back to the last cairn and look again. The route takes about twenty-five minutes each way. Given the inevitable pausing, peering and backtracking required to find the cairns, partial times are redundant, but the following waypoints were taken at roughly five minute intervals.

At first the path is reasonably clear, passing an outdoor privy and winding between rocks (ESE) to cross two linked clearings (Wp.5). Continuing through the woods (SE), look for a third clearing (Wp.6) a few metres to the right of the main path, where we bear right to pass a lime-kiln. We now follow the cairns in a more southerly direction, passing Wp.7 (solely a GPS bearing, indistinguishable from the surrounding woodland) and steadily descending until, off to our right, we can see a partially ruined watchtower perched on the cliffs (Wp.8). Bearing right (SW), we follow a reasonably clear path down to the tower (Wp.9). The entrance to the cave is a small hole, 15 metres before the tower. We return via the same route. The descent from the sanctuary to the starting point takes about forty minutes.

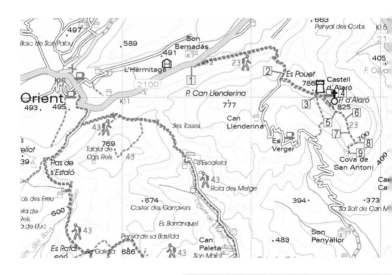

Though two thirds of this walk is featured elsewhere, the new third is so very enjoyable, it merits an itinerary number of its own. Following a glorious trail, we traverse the **Serra d'en Massot**, an unassuming little rise sandwiched between the massifs of **Tomir** and **Massanella**. It's a fabulous off-path route, well marked with cairns and blue waymarks, ideal for getting off the beaten track without risk to life, limb or overall reserves of oomph.

Access: by car or (starting from **Lluc**) bus (L330 from **Palma**, L354 from **Alcúdia**, **Pollença**, & **Sóller**, L355 from **Alcúdia** and **Pollença**). We start from the gates of the **Binifaldó** bottling plant at the **Coll des Pedregaret** (Wp.1) 2.9km from km17.4 of the MA-10. NOTE: the main gates on the MA-10 are closed at weekends. If doing this walk at the weekend or arriving by bus, you can reach Wp.1 by any of the following four options:

(i)   walk up the access road from km17.4 of the MA-10 (quickest option);
(ii)   follow Walk 52 from **Lluc** (most logical for the return);
(iii)   follow Walk 9 from **Lluc** (longest and most attractive);
(iv)   follow Walk 9 from the **Menut Área Recreativa** (Wp.4 of Walk 9) (short and attractive).

mossy oak

Starting from the gates of the **Binifaldó** bottling plant (only accessible by car on working days) (Wp.1 0M), we cross the stone-stepped stile, as if following the GR to **Lluc**, then immediately leave the GR, taking the broad dirt track descending to the south through attractive, moss mantled woodland. After a

off path

steady descent, the track swings sharp right at a small bridge/ford (Wp.16 of Walk 32) (Wp.2 15M). Walk 32 descends into the bed of the torrent at this point, but for the present itinerary, we maintain our southerly direction on a cairn-marked path forking off the track and climbing above the right bank of the torrent.

After crossing a small rise, the path dips down and disappears amid rough rock. On the far side of the dip, we climb onto a limestone shoulder where cairns and blue waymarks indicate the start of the off-path section.

sculpted by a designing hand (before Wp3)

There are patches of path along the flank of the mountain, but for the most part we're picking our way across a fabulous rockscape of rough limestone, where some of the karstic erosion is so delicate it appears to have been sculpted by a designing hand or to be the fossilized remains of some convoluted invertebrate.

You don't really need to consult the book here, but maintaining a southwesterly direction, we go through an open gateway in a fence thirty metres after the disappearance of the path (Wp.3 24M). As the views over the **Aucanella** valley open out fully, we descend briefly, then follow a contour passing a stony *sitja* (Wp.4 31M) before descending again alongside the foot of a sloping outcrop of rock. 100 metres after a second stone cloaked *sitja*, we pass below a large solitary oak (Wp.5 44M) from where we weave our way through the *carritx* to the bed of the torrent (Wp.17 of Walk 32) (Wp.6 46M). Crossing the torrent, we follow a clear path (SE) to join a stony track less than 100 metres later, where we turn right (Wp.7).

The track traverses a wilderness of spurge, mastic and scrubby holm oak then climbs steadily before dwindling to a trail (Wp.8 61M), which continues to climb briefly alongside a tumbledown wall before dipping back into dense woodland. The trail climbs through the woods, broadening to a rough forestry track which we follow until it joins the GR at a wayposted junction (Wp.9 81M), where we turn right. We now simply follow the GR back to **Binifaldó**, forking right at a Y-junction of tracks (Wp.10 82M) and left above an S-bend (Wp.11 91M), to end with an agreeable stroll on a sinuous footpath winding through the woods.

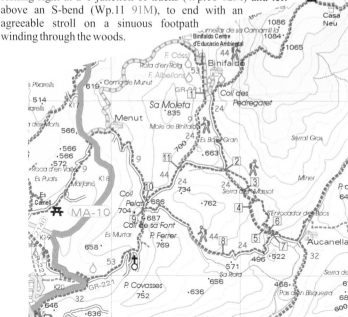

Puig de María

Don't be fooled by the insignificant looking squiggle representing this walk on the map, nor by the fact that most of it is on a road. This glorious little excursion is ideal on a blustery winter's day when it would be unwise to tackle a wilder landscape. Our objective is the **Santuari de la Mare de Deu des Puig**, home to various religious houses from 1348 to 1988, nowadays a bar-restaurant-refuge.

3 | 1H 10M * | 4 km | 300m / 300m | out & back | 5

* return, + 30M for exploring

Access: on foot from **Pollença**. We start at km 52 of the MA-2200, also the **Pollença** by-pass, on a tarmac lane signposted 'Puig de Maria' (Wp.1 0M). If starting on foot from **Pollença**, find the Repsol petrol station (signposted throughout the town as 'Benzinera'), then take the cul-de-sac to the right of the Renault concession and cut across the wasteland onto a lane that leads to a derelict house in front of Wp.1.

Following the tarmac lane, we bear right after 100 metres, from where we already have fine views of the higher mountains behind **Pollença**. After climbing steadily for ten minutes, the tarmac gives way to concrete and we pass the green gates of the last house. Ignoring the water-erosion 'shortcuts' (the road is steep enough), we continue climbing through mixed woodland, passing occasional red crosses daubed on the trees - waymarks for pilgrims, not walkers. The road ends (Wp.2 25M) in a tiny turning circle (room for three small cars, but usually full) and we continue on the restored, neatly cobbled, donkey trail with fine views south towards **Puig de Sant Martí** (see Walk 34). One hundred metres before the sanctuary, we ignore a signposted turning to the left (our return route). At the sanctuary, we can either bear right to go directly to the chapel or continue left of the main walls and go through its *Área Recreativa* (Wp.3 35M) to the impressive refectory. In either case, it's worth spending half an hour exploring.

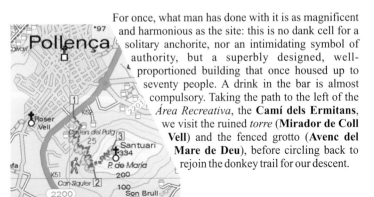

For once, what man has done with it is as magnificent and harmonious as the site: this is no dank cell for a solitary anchorite, nor an intimidating symbol of authority, but a superbly designed, well-proportioned building that once housed up to seventy people. A drink in the bar is almost compulsory. Taking the path to the left of the *Área Recreativa*, the **Camí dels Ermitans**, we visit the ruined *torre* (**Mirador de Coll Vell**) and the fenced grotto (**Avenc del Mare de Deu**), before circling back to rejoin the donkey trail for our descent.

El Fumat is said to have got its name because it was a natural place to stop and have a smoke en route from the **Cala Murta** supply boat to the **Formentor** lighthouse. Nowadays, even non-smokers are drawn to its commanding heights and it has become a well known feature of the drive along the peninsula, not least because the new road goes right through it. **Cala en Gossalba**, though surprisingly little visited, is also well known.

Our descent, however, from **El Fumat** to the *cala* via the dry **Torrent de les Agulles** doesn't appear in any other guidebook I've seen, which is quite inexplicable as it's a lovely wild little walk and makes a far more satisfying circuit than the traditional scramble over **Roca Blanca**.

Despite its intimidating aspect, **El Fumat** is a relatively easy climb, and though our descent crosses rough, pathless ground, it poses no problems so long as you're sure-footed and well-shod. The complete circuit would be a good excursion for a family with venturesome adolescents. Not recommended when it's wet or very hot.

* Short Version 1¾ h

Short Version Excluding **El Fumat**	**Stroll** To **Cala en Gossalba** and back via our return route. The path down, which isn't immediately visible from the *mirador*, starts 10 metres before the metal crash barriers on the right (direction **Cap Formentor**).

Access: by car. Park at the small *mirador* shortly before km 15 of the MA-2210. Best to get there early as there's only room for three or four cars. There's space for one car back towards the tunnel, just before the bend.

From the *mirador* (Wp.1 0M) we walk back along the road towards the tunnel, soon coming into view of **El Fumat**. 100 metres from the sign announcing the tunnel, a large wooden sign for 'Cami Vell del Far' indicates where we scramble up off the road (Wp.2 10M) on a narrow path leading to the remains of the old donkey-trail (clearly zigzagging up to **Coll de la Creu** in the distance) formerly used to supply the lighthouse. A gentle climb along the donkey trail brings us onto the *coll* (Wp.3 25M), where we see the path zigzagging down from the pass above the **Cala Murta** valley.

N.B. It is possible to reach the *coll* via the stairs on the **Pollença** side of the tunnel: this should only be attempted by men 'super, spider, or bat', as sheer drops mean one needs to be able to fly or cling to the rock like a limpet.

At the western end of the *coll*, red waymarks and cairns indicate the way up to **El Fumat**. Clear, easy walking up small patches of scree, some so well trodden it's almost a path, and sloping rock shelves, brings us to the base of the peak, where we bear left towards **Alcúdia** to follow the waymarks round the rocks to the top (Wp.4 40M).

Returning to the *coll*, we continue on the donkey trail, zigzagging down toward the head of **Torrent de les Agulles**, where there's a 50 metre level stretch, at either end of which two clear but narrow runoff channels feed into the main torrent. Leaving the path at the first of these channels (Wp.5 55M), we descend alongside the watershed, picking our way across *carritx* covered debris. We soon come to a reassuring cairn at the crux of the two runoff channels. We then follow a rough path through the *carritx*, to the junction with a second, larger runoff channel, where we take to the bed of the torrent.

Cala en Gossalba

And that's pretty much it. Unless you're feeling in an unusually perverse mood, you can't really get lost down here, and we just keep on keeping on down the torrent, hopping from rock to rock, skirting the occasional fallen pine, but always staying in or near the bed. The rocks get larger, the landscape wilder the lower we go, passing some superb rock formations as we approach the declivity of the *cala*.

Within sight of the sea, we reach a final little rock shelf that's easily descended, though you may need to slide on your bottom for a moment, before eventually emerging on a tiny stony beach backed by crystal clear waters (Wp.6 100M).

To return to our starting point, we scramble onto the rocks on our left, where cairns indicate our route over to the neighbouring beach (105M). The way up from the easternmost beach is along a good path criss-crossing the **Canal de Cala en Gossalba** torrent and winding through the remains of a pine forest before climbing back to the road (130M).

The small peak of **Na Bauçana** (also known as **Bauza**) probably enjoys more prominence per metre than any other summit on the island. Despite it's relatively modest height (614 metres) it's a landmark for miles around, its wooded dome clearly visible from most of our southern itineraries.

More importantly in walking terms, the scope of the views from the top is almost unique, including the **Na Burguesa** ridge, the **Garrafa** plateau, the peaks behind **Sa Trapa**, **S'Esclop**, **Galatzó**, **Es Puntals**, **Planicia**, the **Fita del Ram** - in fact, just about everything all the way to **Puig Major** and **Massanella** in the east. Hardly any other viewing point boasts quite such an encompassing outlook. The walk is mainly on good dirt tracks and only earns a high exertion rating for the steep path at the end.

Access: by car. The walk starts at the entrance to the **Son Cortey** estate on the **Coll des Molí de Vent** at km 8.3 of the PMV1032 between **Puigpunyent** and **Galilea**. There's parking for one car immediately west of the **Son Cortey** gate and two to the east.

Ignoring the double-gates of the entrance into **Son Cortey**, we take a track on the left marked with a walking signpost for 'Calvià' and blocked to vehicles by a metal latticework gate (Wp.1 0M). We cross the gate via a ladder stile, then immediately veer right, after which we maintain a southerly direction at an inverted Y-junction (Wp.2) and ignore a branch descending to the right (Wp.3). At the next Y-junction (Wp.4 11M), the **Calvià** trail forks right (signposted 'Calvià 1h25'), but we stay on the main track. Seventy-five

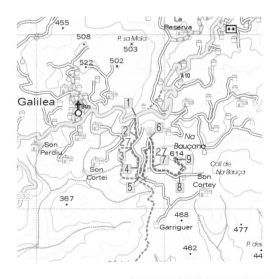

metres later we double back to the left (Wp.5 the track straight ahead is ornamented with a sign explicitly prohibiting walkers), climbing NNE.

The track passes two lime-kilns and becomes narrower as it climbs through an extraordinary profusion of strawberry trees. At a natural *mirador* overlooking **Galilea** (Wp.6), the track veers back to the south-east, soon passing a narrow, cairn-marked path (Wp.7 27M) on the right descending ten metres to a well-preserved charcoal burners' hut with an unusual, paved *sitja*. Curving round to the south of **Na Bauçana**, we cross a wall and pass a second cabin/*sitja* as we climb across a grassy rise. Shortly after passing a large waymarking arrow pieced together from rocks, we leave the track, forking left (Wp.8 38M) on a clearly defined cairn-marked trail (NNE).

The trail soon dwindles to a path, climbing steeply through the woods, crossing frequent steps of roughly tailored stone.

The stepped path to the summit

In case you're wondering what such a well-made path is doing going nowhere very practical, this itinerary dates from the early nineteenth century when hiking or *excursionisme* was integral to resurgent Catalán and Mallorcan nationalisms, a means of both expressing identity and claiming one's homeland, in the course of which many classic walking routes were either trailblazed or tailored, including **Massanella**, **Sa Trapa**, **Puig Tomir**, **Puig d'en Farineta**, the **Pas Vermell** and the present itinerary.

After a steady to steep climb, we eventually wind across bare rock to the trig-point (Wp.9 52M) for views that give the lie to the summit's diminutive size. We return by the same route.

The **Camí des Pescadors** (or **Fishermen's Path**) and the **Camí Sa Volta des General** (**The General's Tour**), named after the local aristocrat for whom it was constructed, are two of the great 'commuting' paths of the northwest and combine to make a near perfect day's hiking, including fabulous sea views, charming woodland paths, a wild coastline, a grand manor house, daunting cliffs and a good dose of domesticity in the welcome guise of the bars and restaurants of **Port des Canonge** and **Banyalbufar**. I say 'almost' because it's a linear walk and I prefer circuits, but if you're feeling energetic this minor imperfection can be remedied by returning to **Esporles** on the **Camí des Correu** (see Walk 47). For the most part, the route is well wayposted.

Access: on foot from **Esporles**, return on foot via Walk 47 or by bus L200 (currently running at 15.35, 17.15, 18.45, 20.00). If you're staying in **Banyalbufar**, the morning bus to **Esporles** currently departs at 7.10, 8.40, 9.50, 11.10.

Esporles

Starting in front of **Esporles** church (Wp.1 0M), we take **Carrer Nou San Pere**, crossing the *torrent* of the same name and **Carrer Major**. The next turning on the left, **Carrer Pont**, leads briefly into **Carrer de Sa Costeta**, where we bear left on **Carrer de sa Pansa**, the nameplate of which is partially obscured by ivy.

We then turn right on **Carrer s'Avenc**, which ends in a car-park (Wp.2 10M) where we take a dirt track to the north. Ignoring all branches, we follow the main track as it climbs gently across the **Costa de son Dameto**. At a Y-junction where there's a large rock in the crux of the Y with 'Es Noguera' painted on it (Wp.3 30M), we bear left, staying on the main track. The track climbs past scattered cottages and cabins, passing a branch for **Can Covent** (Wp.4), after which it dwindles to a trail leading to a triple junction of tracks (Wp.5 50M). Ignoring a concrete track descending to the left, we bear left along the main dirt track, passing the entrance to **Can Pastor**. Forking left 100 metres later (Wp.6), we descend behind a house to a path that leads to the C710 (Wp.7 55M).

Turning left we follow the road for fifty metres, passing the km 79 post. At a wayposted crossroads (Wp.8) with a dirt track just below a blue 40km speed limit sign, we turn right on the branch of the track heading north. Near the start and at the end of this track you will see small 'Camino Privado Prohibido El Paso' signs. Ignore these. This is a well-used, official path, wayposted by the local authorities, and residents en route assured us there was no problem. At the end of the track, we go through a gate to the walled area and small *mirador* at **Mirant del Mar** (Wp.9 75M).

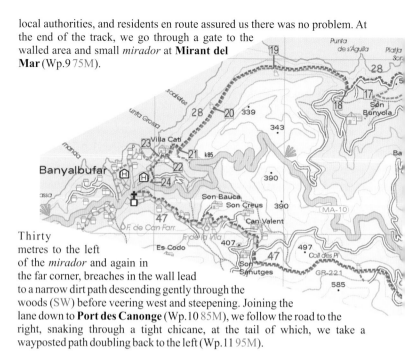

Thirty metres to the left of the *mirador* and again in the far corner, breaches in the wall lead to a narrow dirt path descending gently through the woods (SW) before veering west and steepening. Joining the lane down to **Port des Canonge** (Wp.10 85M), we follow the road to the right, snaking through a tight chicane, at the tail of which, we take a wayposted path doubling back to the left (Wp.11 95M).

This is perhaps the loveliest part of the **Camí des Pescadors** as we descend through the **Son Coll** woods, principally oak, but also pine and laurel. On reaching a bend in a broad trail (Wp.12 105M), we continue descending to join a dirt track, also on a bend (Wp.13 110M). Twenty metres to the left, a waypost indicates a slithery descent to recover the path as it runs alongside a dry torrent. At the junction with the next dirt track (Wp.14 115M), we turn right to rejoin the tarmac road fifty metres later. We now follow the road down to the coast, passing en route the **Can Madó** and **Can Toni Moreno** restaurants.

At the T-junction above the bay (Wp.15 130M), we turn left down to the parking area, from the end of which, we can see, seventy-five metres to the left, an isolated signpost indicating 'Banyalbufar 1h20'. Bearing left through the gateway at the end of the car-park, we follow the signposted route, crossing a small gully and climbing through the woods behind the seafront. After descending into a second, larger gully lined with abandoned fishermen's shanties, we climb a short flight of steps, beyond which wayposts lead us through a maze of interlinking tracks, trails and paths to join the end of a very broad dirt track in front of double wooden gates (Wp.16 140M).

We follow this dirt track west, towards the **Es Corral Fals** cliffs, climbing steadily along the boundary line of the **Son Bunyola** estate, now owned by Richard Branson. Within sight of the immense manor house (so very immense one can only pray the man has lots of friends), we bear right at a Y-junction (Wp.17 155M). One hundred and fifty metres later, having already passed a first branch on the left, we bear right at a triple junction (Wp.18) to follow a broad signposted trail curving round below the bulging cliffs of **Es Corral Fals** from where we have superb views over the **Punta de s'Àguila**.

Port des Canonge

If the woodland path behind the port is the prettiest part of the walk, this is far and away the most impressive, the great mass of molten-looking rock looming above

us, the occasional half-ton block lying below the path where it's fallen! If you want to put things into perspective or feel the need to dwarf human vanity, come here and scurry past quickly - you feel very small, indeed.

After that humbling little passage, our route becomes a classic Mallorcan corniche trail. Strolling through pine woods backed by the deep blue sea (green and blue really ought to be the colours of the island's flag), we pass a lime-kiln (Wp.19 175M) and a small ruin (Wp.20 190M). Ignoring a major trail descending toward the coast, we go through old iron gates, 150 metres after which, directly behind the house of **Sa Cabarola**, we leave the main trail (Wp.21 200M).

The main trail leads round to the **Volta des General** bend in the C710, a popular starting point for the descent to **Port des Canonge**, but to avoid a kilometre on the main road, we turn sharp right behind **Sa Cabarola** on a narrow path initially heading in a northerly direction. The path then zigzags down (SW) to a sharp right hand bend (Wp.22 205M), where we descend onto a well trodden way winding steeply through palmetto, *carritx* and pine to join a narrow track directly behind a flat-roofed house overlooking **Port de Banyalbufar** (Wp.23 215M). Bearing left, we join a roughly surfaced lane, the **Camí de sa Galera**, which we follow up to the village. After a brief steep climb, we reach the main road in front of the **Hotel Mar i Vent** (Wp.24 225M). The bus-stop and the start of the **Camí des Correu** (Walk 47) are two hundred metres to the west.

29 THREE VILLAGES + ONE THUNDERING GREAT CLIMB

Essentially, this itinerary is two loops tacked onto one another and can easily be broken into several smaller walks. The basic loop is the classic tour from **Sóller** of **Binibassi**, **Fornalutx** and **Biniaraix**, a lovely, bucolic stroll that should be within everyone's range. On top of that, the energetic have the option of climbing a superb donkey trail to **Sa Bassa** and the **Mirador de ses Barques**, from where another donkey trail brings us back to **Fornalutx**. The climb to **Sa Bassa** is via the **Camí de s'Alzina Fumadora**, named after a large, shady Holm Oak under which everyone used to stop for a fag break.

4*   4H**   14 km   500m / 500m   ↻   5

*Short Versions (a) 4, (b) 2   **Short Versions (a) 3hours, (b) 1½ hours

---

Short Version:- There's an interesting short walk to be done linking the present itinerary with Walk 7. Follow Walk 7 to Wp.4. Turn right, then fork left 30-metres later to join a lovely path that follows a contour for a little over 30M before emerging on the MA-10 at the junction with the **Fornalutx** road. 50 metres down the **Fornalutx** road we join the present itinerary just above Wp.8.

Access: on foot from **Sóller**

From **Sóller's** central **Plaza de sa Constitució**, we take **Carrer de sa Lluna** next to the BBVA bank, then turn second left on **Carrer de la Victoria 11 Maig**. Carrying straight on at the crossroads, we bear right at the bridge (signposted 'Piscina Municipal') into **Avenguda d'Asturies**, then turn right at the football field on the **Biniaraix/Fornalutx** road (Wp.1 10M). When the road crosses **Pont de Can Rave**, we turn left on a tarmac lane (following the GR), which promptly swings right, passing two signposted branches (see Walk 7).

Bearing left at the end of the lane (Wp.2 25M), we climb a partially cobbled trail to the idyllic hamlet of **Binibassi**. Ignoring the access road, we bear left (signposted 'Fornalutx') beside a trough-like culvert to take the footpath out of the hamlet.

Approaching Binibassi

After going through a green gate, we follow a broad trail across terraces before bearing right at a waypost to take a narrow path marked with red dots. We immediately go through another gate and bear right down a stepped descent onto a path running alongside a high retaining wall.

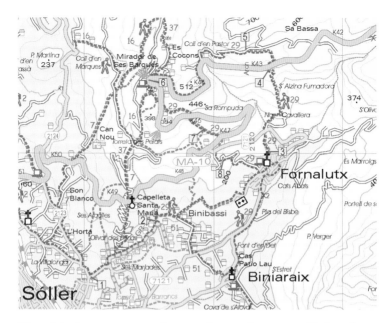

The path leads onto a tarmac and concrete lane passing terraces. The lane dips then climbs past the **Fornalutx** cemetery before leading into the village itself (45M). Ignoring the road descending to the right, we continue straight ahead, passing the kindergarten to join **Carrer de Sol**, from where **Carrer de sa Plaza** leads into the main village square (50M). If you don't intend doing the full walk, return to **Carrer de Sol** after exploring the village.

For the full walk

We climb the steps next to **Fornalutx** church and, from **Carrer des Vent**, take **Carrer de Tramuntana** up to the **Camí de s'Alzina Fumadora / Sa Comuna** (Wp.3 55M). Climbing past hillside smallholdings, we cross the **Fornalutx** access road, where we pass above a small fenced reservoir and take a concrete track, 30 metres along which, a signpost indicates our donkey trail on the left.

Camí de s'Alzina Fumadora

For the next half-hour, we simply follow the cobbled trail, if something that climbs so relentlessly can be described as 'simple'. The long, shallow steps look easy, but they're deceptively steep and there's every chance you'll reach the top wishing never to see another step again.

However, the effort is amply rewarded with superb views across the intricate jigsaw of terraces climbing towards the **Ofre** ridge to the south. After crossing an access track, we climb steadily to go through a wire gate. The climb gets even steeper, passing a waypost and zigzagging up across terraces, before finally emerging on the MA-10, just east of km 43 at a signpost for 'Fornalutx 45M' (Wp.4 90M).

Fifty metres to the right, we take a signposted path ('Pla de sa Bassa') crossing a stile then a *sitja*, where the path broadens to a trail climbing to join a rough dirt track behind a green fire-fighting reservoir (Wp.5 105M). Turning left, we follow the track round the base of **Sa Bassa**, going through the natural gateway of **Coll d'en Pastor**, before descending through rubble strewn switchbacks to one of the **Es Cocons** access gates. We bear left, down to a second gate, possibly locked but an easy climb over the left hand pillar, onto the MA-10 at km 43.7.

Unfortunately, we now have over a kilometre on the road to descend to the **Mirador de ses Barques**. At the *mirador* car park, we cross onto the right hand side of the road and, as the road bears left, go through the gap between the stone and metal crash barriers (Wp.6 140M), just behind which a signpost indicates the common start of the **Sóller/Fornalutx/Port de Sóller** paths.

After descending along a narrow path with a steel cable handrail, we go through a bedstead gate and turn left to rejoin the MA-10 100 metres later. 150 metres along the road, we bear left on a dirt track signposted 'Fornalutx/Costa d'en Nico'. The track passes two houses before being blocked by a gate, where we turn right to join the cobbled donkey trail down to **Fornalutx**. The first narrow stretch descends directly to the road. 50 metres to the left, we take a signposted concrete track for 10 metres until a waypost indicates the next stage of the donkey trail descending to our left. Taking care not to drift off onto the terraces, we follow the donkey trail until it runs into a broader stony track (Wp.7 170M). We bear left for 30 metres before branching right on cobbled steps to cut out a bend. 50 metres further along the track, another section of donkey trail cuts out a second bend, after which the track descends to cross the MA-10 (173M) for the last time.

On the other side of the road, we follow a concrete driveway behind a house then cross the gravelled area in front of a carport. We then cross the **Fornalutx** access road onto a tarmac lane, which we follow till a waypost (Wp.8 180M) indicates a shortcut avoiding a bend. We now repeat this procedure, following and crossing the lane five times. Behind the first house on the outskirts of **Fornalutx**, we leave the lane and take the steps behind the house down to **Carrer de la Pau**. Bearing left we come back to **Carrer de Sol**.

To return to Sóller from Fornalutx
We turn right on **Carrer de Sol** and descend to the main road in front of the principal **Fornalutx** car-park. Bearing right, we follow the road past the **Per Amunt Restaurant**, then bear left on **Carrer Mallorca** (signposted 'Sóller a Peu'), cutting a bend in the road. After a second shortcut lane, we follow the road for 500 metres, taking the second turning on the left, a narrow lane that brings us into **Biniaraix** (210M). Turning right on the **Carrer de Sant Josep**, we walk through the small square in front of the bar/bodega and follow the 'Sóller a Peu' signs before steps lead down to the road, which we follow back to **Sóller** (225M). Ignoring traffic signs suggesting the town centre is on our right (it ain't), we carry straight on to rejoin **Carrer de sa Lluna**.

At first glance, **Sa Rateta**, the scruffy rock south of the **Cúber Reservoir**, is as mousy as its name suggests, a rather furtive rise with no distinguishing crown and no very apparent way to the top.

Sa Rateta & Ofre from the MA10

Yet it's one of my favourite little mountains in Mallorca, a wonderfully wild and isolated spot with commanding views of the more majestic summits surrounding it, so it was a pleasure to return for this revised version of our original walk. The itinerary is only recommended for experienced walkers, as it traverses rough, frequently pathless terrain.

| 4 | 3½ H | 10.5 km | 450m / 450m | ↻ | 0 |

| **Stroll**: | **Extension**: |
| as per Walk 18 | **L'Ofre** (see Walk 18) |

Access: by car or bus (L354 seasonal service between **Sóller** and **Alcúdia**). Our itinerary starts at the **Cúber** parking area/bus stop at km34 of the MA10.

From the **Cúber** parking area (Wp.1 0M), we take the tarmac track alongside the reservoir then turn left just before the dam (Wp.2 11M) on a rough track that soon dwindles to a trail climbing across a rise, where the **Torrent d'Almedra** gorge opens out before us. On the far side of the torrent, we can see an interred aquifer rising toward a bulging cliff on the right, which is where the present itinerary diverges from Walk 31.

After dropping down to cross the torrent, we climb to the cliff, immediately below which cairns and the word 'Rateta' daubed in red on the concrete wall indicate where our path climbs to the right (Wp.3 26M). Though not visible from below, the path almost immediately becomes clear, long cobbled sections zigzagging up for 50 metres, after which the gradient eases. Following cairns and occasional red dots, we cross a *sitja*, 20 metres after which there is a waymarked fork (Wp.4 33M).

Ignoring the branch to the right, we maintain direction (S), climbing across sheets of rock and patches of path to the **Coll d'es Bosc**, where green painted letters on the right indicate the ongoing route for **Rateta** (Wp.5 41M).

At first, for anyone with an affinity for paths, the prospect is not promising, but if you look up toward the folds of rock, you will see the sloping margins of a retaining wall defining a snow gatherers' donkey trail. Following the cairnmarked route, we climb across the rocks to join the donkey trail just above a tailored chicane (Wp.6 50M).

on the donkey trail

We now simply follow the cobbled trail and the route indicated by cairns when the trail becomes obscure, pausing to enjoy fine views of the **Alaró** and **Alcaldena** summits to the south.

Following a steady climb, the donkey trail swings right (Wp.7) on a slightly obscure stretch before resuming its westerly course. After traversing an area of bare rock (Wp.8 58M), we wade through a shallow swale of *carritx* to reach the foot of the last tailored stretch (Wp.9 71M), which leads us to the roofless ruin of a snow gatherers' cabin (Wp.10 75M) and the end of anything very pathlike.

Various cairn-marked routes climb to the ridge from here, the clearest heading due north to reach the first of several small summits (Wp.11 80M). Bearing left across sheets of limestone, we traverse the main summit, staying on the nearside of the ridge and heading in a southwesterly direction until a clear patch of path (Wp.12 85M) indicates where we veer further left, away from the ridge, to follow a cairn-marked route down to the **Coll d'es Gats** (Wp.13 98M).

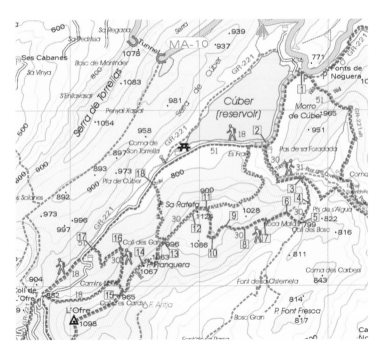

If you need an escape route, it is possible to cross the wall here and follow a very faint sheep trail marked with cairns down to the north, into the **Ofre** valley.

admiring the views

The cairns disappear after 150 metres and the trail splinters into a confusing web of ways, but winding through the *carritx* in a northerly direction and aiming to pass to the right of the stand of pine at the bottom of the slope, you will come to a broken down fence punctured with numerous rambler-sized holes (Wp.18).

The descent takes about 15 minutes and joins the main track a little over half an hour from the start.

NOTE: a solitary cairn at the bottom suggests the 'approved' descent is straight down the slope in a northwesterly direction, but a traverse is gentler on the knees.

To continue along the ridge from **Coll d'es Gats**, we stay on the near side of the wall and bear left at the southwestern end of the coll to follow a faint, cairn-marked way skirting behind the obvious (very obvious!) crag blocking direct progress. Natural 'steps' in the rock bring us back onto the ridge, where we bear left and, staying well back from the cliffs, climb to the small **Franquera** summits (Wp.14 118M). Our next objective is a wall, only the head of which is visible at first, making it look like a cabin. Crossing the wall 15 metres from its upper end, we descend (SW) along a steep, stony way to reach the **Coll d'es Cards** (Wp.15 133M). Which is where we intersect with Walk 18.

To return to **Cúber**, we head north, crossing a broken wall to take a clear path down to a Y-junction. Continuing straight on (the right hand branch), we bear right at the next metal pylon and descend steadily through the pine, passing occasional cairns before emerging at a large *sitja* (Wp.16 143M). Bearing left (SW) on a broad trail, we descend to a trickling stream and large trough beside a stand of poplars. Taking the fainter of the two cow paths on the eastern side of the stream, we meander down, crossing a tangle of paths, half-paths and runoff channels, to emerge on the **Ofre** dirt track opposite a small byre (Wp.17 158M). Turning right, we follow the dirt track back to **Cúber**, returning to the start either via the GR on the northern side of the reservoir or via the tarmac track to the south.

31 CÚBER: TOSSALS VERDS

This adventurous excursion takes us through five rough tunnels piping water down from the **Cúber** reservoir, visits Mallorca's first manned and still most popular refuge, and circles the **Tossals Verds** massif along shady charcoal-burning paths. It's possible to cross all except the second tunnel without a torch (if you don't mind not seeing where you put your feet), but not recommended. During the descent, you will see painted signs announcing a toll for the privilege of crossing the **Sólleric** estate. I've not heard of anyone actually being asked to pay.

*** The refuge (open all year) and has dormitory accommodation for 30. Book even for eating, as it's popular with large parties (Tel: 971 173700 or 971 173701).

Access: by car and bus (L354 from **Alcúdia**, **Pollença**, & **Sóller**). The walk starts from the **Font des Noguer Área Recreativa** just west of km34 of the MA10. If arriving by car, park in the **Font des Noguer Área Recreativa** car park. If arriving by bus, ask to be dropped off at **Cúber**. An alternative access to this route is via the refuge service road from the south (see Tour & Trail map). The last 2.5km open to cars are a bit pot-holey, but thereafter it's an attractive stroll through the gorge. The other advantage is that parking here is less risky than at the top end, which is notorious for car break-ins.

Starting from the **Área Recreative de Sa Font des Noguera** at km33.8 of the MA-10 (Wp.1 0M), we cross the stile at the western end of the car-park and follow the GR to **Cúber**, where we take the tarmac track along the southern side of the reservoir. When the tarmac track swings right to cross the dam wall (Wp.2 10M), we bear left on a dirt track. The track soon narrows to a walking trail descending steeply on loose stones and <u>passing</u> a tunnel with a concrete pipe running through it - this is NOT one of our tunnels. Ten minutes from the dam wall we cross a torrent, then follow the course of the large, occasionally interred concrete water-pipe, along an easy dirt path. A steady then gentle climb brings us through a cutting onto a small plateau littered with sections of discarded piping. Descending from the plateau, gently at first then more steeply along a rough, rock strewn path, we come to the first of the tunnels (on our right), dubbed 'Sóllerich Paso', (Wp.3 40M).

The first tunnel is easy, the second less so: you can't see the exit, the ground's rough, it dips down at the end, and you have to be careful not to clout your head on the roof. After a much longer descent, we come to the third tunnel, which has a low entrance, but is in fact easier than the first two with a well beaten path and large window halfway along. The fourth is little more than an archway, the fifth and last has been roughly gated. Leaving the fifth tunnel (Wp.4 65M) we bear right on a rough track (direction 'Sals'). After ten minutes, we ignore a branch on the right and continue on the main track for a steady descent to a large metal gate and ladder-stile leading to a small wooden bridge (Wp.5 80M). Crossing the bridge, we join the tarmac lane from **Almedrà**. After climbing up the lane for ten minutes, we bear right at a signpost indicating the refuge is a further ten minutes away, and follow a

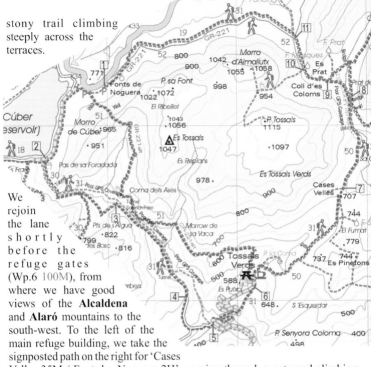

stony trail climbing steeply across the terraces.

We rejoin the lane shortly before the refuge gates (Wp.6 100M), from where we have good views of the **Alcaldena** and **Alaró** mountains to the south-west. To the left of the main refuge building, we take the signposted path on the right for 'Cases Velles 35M / Font des Noguera 2H', passing through a gate and climbing across terraces. A steady then gentle climb with fine views of the terraced valley below **Cases Velles**, passes first a large pine tree (to our left), **El Fumat**, reputedly the largest of its kind in the region, then a signposted path on the right for **Mancor des Valles** (not recommended). A path to the left (Wp.7 140M) a few metres before a GR waypost, leads to the terraces below **Cases Velles**, where there are innumerable fine picnic spots.

Continuing along the main path, we circle **Tossals Verds**, passing the celebrated **Canaleta de Massanella** (see Walk 19), before crossing and re-crossing the stream just below it (Wp.8 200M). A gentle climb brings us past the turning for **Massanella** and **Lluc**, signposted 'Font d'es Prat' (Wp.9 205M) and the branch to **Puig de Tossals Verds** (Wp.10 210M).

Crossing at Wp.8

We then cross **Coll d'es Colloms** for a steady descent along a roughly cobbled trail down to a gate and a bridge over the new concrete *canaleta* (Wp.11 225M). Bearing left, we walk alongside the *canaleta* (doubtless on a hot day wishing we were IN it) back to our starting point in a little over thirty minutes.

Despite its length, this circuit is relatively easy and only earns an exertion rating of 4 for the rock-hopping in the riverbed. The scenery is very varied, but the more remarkable variety is in what we walk in and on: roads, lanes, a paved pilgrims' way, concrete tracks, cart tracks, dirt tracks, cobbled paths, *carritx*-covered ways, a limestone maze, the bed of a torrent… you name it, we walk it, excepting motorways and airport runways. The ascent on the **Camí Vell** from **Caimari** is easy and poses no difficulties. The descent, however, via the **Torrent des Picarols** should not be undertaken in wet weather (there's little risk of flooding, but the rocks might be slippery). Pathfinding is a problem between Wps.17 & 21. Long trousers or pedal-pushers are preferable to shorts between Wps. 19 & 22. Start early to avoid the improbably large coaches that plough up and down the MA-2130.

| 4* | 5½-6H ** | 20 km | 550m / 550m | ↻ | 3 |

* Short Versions 3
** Short Versions **(a)** 2h **(b)** 4h **(c)** 2h (all estimated)

Short Versions	Stroll
(a) to **Lluc via Camí Vell**, returning by bus **(b)** bus to **Lluc** and descend via **Aucanella** **(c)** bus to **Lluc**, descend via **Camí Vell** (from the *fuente* at the top of the car-park)	Though it's a dreary slog at the end of a long walk, the lane between **Caimari** and **Binibona** might make a pleasant stroll on a fresh day. The **Carrer de Binibona** starts just below the smaller church at the top of **Caimari**.

Access: on foot from **Caimari** (accessible by bus L330 from **Palma**). There's a large car-park on the MA-2130 at the northern end of **Caimari**. If two cars are available, you may wish to leave one at **Binibona** or the **Albellons Hotel**, thus avoiding the hot trudge along the tarmac at the end.

From the northern end of **Caimari** (Wp.1 0M), we follow the MA-2130 for 400 metres to the *mirador* at the first U-bend, where the **Camí Vell de Lluc** begins (Wp.2 5M). Climbing the broad track from the *mirador*, we bear right at a Y-junction (Wp.3 15M) on stairs leading to the main road, which we parallel for a while then cross (Wp.4 25M) to climb steeply on a newly paved section of the **Camí Vell**.

After passing the **Son Canta** farmhouse, we bear left (Wp.5 35M) on a new path descending alongside the road to the **Sa Coveta Área Recreativa**, where we go through a tunnel under the road (Wps.6 40M) and cross a stile to reach the start of a dirt track. We climb gently past a memorial to 'Isabel Morel Morro' (Wp.7 48M), then steeply to a junction where the main track, marked with a GR waypost, doubles back to the right (Wp.8 53M). Sticking with the GR and the steep climb, we cross a *coll* before descending to a signposted junction at the foot of a long, straight stretch of cobbling (Wp.9 70M). As you climb this cobbled stretch, it's worth looking down on the valley below us

(SE). The small, wooded, conical mountain in the middle is **Puig Mitja**. Our return route is on the far side of this mountain.

The track narrows on a fully cobbled stretch climbing to a natural limestone gateway (Wp.10 85M) where it levels off before passing a large new building and, 20 metres later, a massive oak tree (Wp.11 90M).

A gentle descent brings us to a crossroads of dirt tracks, where we maintain direction (NW) down to the main road (Wp.12 95M), 75 metres from the **Coll de sa Bataia** petrol station and bar/restaurant, where I suggest you take any refreshment you haven't got in your backpack: the coffee's not great, but the welcome is infinitely warmer than in the bars at **Lluc**.

Camí Vell de Lluc

50 metres north of the garage, we turn right on the road to **Lluc**. The **Camí Vell** descends to the left, but unless you have a strong compulsion to light a candle or catch a bus, there's little point going down to **Lluc** itself and I suggest you stay on the main road for 500 metres and, just after the first left-hand bend, take the GR-221 to the right, signposted 'Binifaldó/Pollença' (Wp.13 110M). N.B. this path joins the dirt track starting just before the bend, so you could take the dirt track immediately.

Thirty metres from the road, we bear right at a waypost and small bridge to cross a deforested area and join the dirt track from the gates. The track goes through a gap in a wall, where it narrows and starts to climb, crossing a watercourse before swinging round to join another track. Ignoring all branch tracks, we climb steadily, following the wayposts, until the track dwindles to a path (Wp.14 130M), 100 metres after which we cross the **Coll de sa Font**, where there's another 'Binifaldó' signpost. 50 metres after the *coll*, we bear left on another dirt track leading to **Coll Pelat** and the branch track (Wp.15 140M) down to the **Menut** farmhouse (see Walk 9). Bearing <u>right</u>, we continue on the main dirt track, still following the GR, as it descends then climbs slightly to a third, unnamed *coll*. Descending steadily from the *coll*, we stay on the dirt track when the GR bears left onto a narrow path through the woods, and continue descending, soon coming onto a newly concreted stretch. The concrete gives way to partially gravelled dirt descending to a torrent and small bridge/ford, where the track swings left and starts climbing (Wp.16 155M). We leave the track just before the bridge/ford.

The cairn-marked route climbs slightly to the right, away from the torrent, but we descend into the torrent and start walking along its rocky bed, occasionally following a vague path along its right bank. The valley gradually narrows and the side-path eventually disappears under a rockspill, from where we are obliged to follow the bed of the torrent, hopping from rock to rock, occasionally steadying ourselves with our hands. After a little over twenty minutes, we pass two large, shady oaks, the second of which has a *sitja* underneath it.

Sticking to the bed of the torrent, we pass through the remains of a wall, 10 metres after which, we bear left, leaving the stream bed on a broad path marked with two large cairns (Wp.17 190M).

One hundred metres later, we bear left on a very rough dirt track, which we leave after 50 metres, just after a short S-bend, bearing right and heading through the rocks to a line of oaks and a stone gateway (all that remains of an old wall) topped with a cairn.

Going through the gateway, we wind along a natural path defined by outcrops of limestone, passing a large rock pond and crossing the rough dirt track twice, the second time beside a fragile looking waypost indicating 'Ses Figueroles/Binibona' on the right and 'Miner' on the left.

Crossing the track and some low rocks, we follow a cairn-marked way winding through the rocks, bringing us down to the fenced fields of the recently restored **Aucanella** farmhouse, invisible at present but betrayed by a large bank of solar panels to our left. Pathfinding is tricky here, so follow the cairns carefully.

Just above the fenced fields, we bear right on an infinitesimally faint track (Wp.18 210M) for 50 metres, then left to find a faint path through a wall gateway (Wp.19 213M) running alongside a ditch next to the fields.

At the end of the fields, we go through another wall gateway (Wp.20 217M) and bear left to cross the head of the **Torrent des Picarols** onto a faint path densely overgrown with *carritx* (watch out for concealed rocks). Passing behind a 5 metre high boulder, we bear right (S), staying on the level for about 100 metres, after which the path gradually starts to descend, passing occasional cairns.

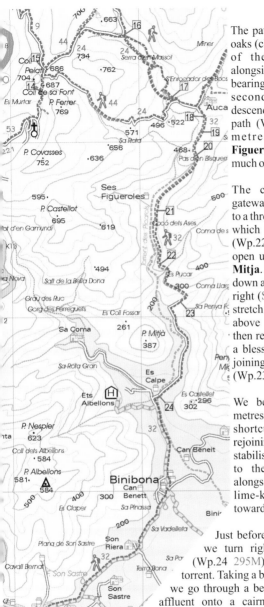

The path passes a large stand of oaks (clearly visible from the top of the *torrent*), then runs alongside an old wall, before bearing away from the wall at a second stand of oaks and descending to a broader, clearer path (Wp.21 240M), about 250 metres south of the **Ses Figueroles** house, visible through much of the descent.

The clear path passes two gateways before climbing gently to a three-bar gate, 50 metres after which we come to a rocky pass (Wp.22 255M) where the views open up round the conical **Puig Mitja**. Bearing left (E), we zigzag down a rocky path before bearing right (S) on a slightly overgrown stretch for a final brief climb above the **Picarols** gorge. We then resume our descent, passing a blessedly shady stretch before joining a badly eroded cart track (Wp.23 275M).

We bear right, then left 100 metres later, where cairns mark a shortcut through the woods, rejoining the track on a better stabilised section. We now stick to the dirt track as it runs alongside the torrent, passing two lime-kilns before descending toward the torrent.

Just before the track starts climbing, we turn right past two large cairns (Wp.24 295M) to cross the bed of the torrent. Taking a broad path on the other side, we go through a bedstead gate, then cross an affluent onto a cairn-marked path up to the partially asphalted access track to **Sa Coma**.

Turning left, we join a tarmac lane next to the driveway to the **Albellons Hotel**, a little under ten minutes from the implausibly tidy hamlet (virtually all hotels) of **Binibona**. Ignoring the main road out of **Binibona**, we take the **Carrer de Caimari/Camí de Binibona** for a rather wearisome trudge along (and sometimes up!) the road back to **Caimari** (330M).

33 RAFAL D'ARIANT & THE MORTITX GORGE

This is the famous twin of Walk 10, a descent into the wild, untenanted land around the abandoned **Rafal d'Ariant** farmhouse. Pathfinding is difficult and the looped return via the **Mortitx Gorge** is only for the adventurous. If you're short of time and value views over sweat sodden T-shirts and hard walking, Walk 10 is a better bet. If you want to be in the heart of the wilderness, this is the walk for you. If you have time for both, the two itineraries complement each other and are both highly recommended

*   linear, 5 if returning via the gorge
**   + 1h for exploring the **Ariant** estate, Short Version 2h20

Extensions: see text.

> **Stroll**
> Take the **l'Havanor** track and turn right at Wp.15 (look for a cairn on the right 5 minutes after Wp.2 of Walk 10) to the head of the gorge.

Access: by car or bus (L354 seasonal service between **Sóller** and **Alcúdia**, request stop). The walk starts from the **Mortitx** farm gates at km10.8 of the MA10. There's adequate roadside parking at the farm gates and 50 metres down the road.

From the farm gates (Wp.1 0M), we follow the driveway track as it passes a tennis court and the main farmhouse. Behind the tennis courts, we ignore a first turning on the right to a tiny bungalow, and take the second right passing a waymarked hut. The track descends between former cherry orchards (most of the trees have recently been uprooted) before veering right then left through a wall - if this is blocked, there's a stile just after the track veers right. We then bear left at a Y-junction and leave the track 30 metres later, turning right on a stony path (Wp.2 10M) badly overgrown with *carritx*.

Winding through the *carritx* and picking our way over outcrops of rock, we pass occasional waymarks and cairns, descending into a large depression dotted with pine trees. If you intend coming back the same way, it's worth glancing back every once in a while to orient yourself for the return. After a gradual descent, we cross a broken fence beside a stile (Wp.3 20M) and continue on a slightly clearer path alongside the fence. Ignoring branches to the right, we cross a low stone retaining wall (Wp.4 25M) and continue alongside the remains of the fence. We then cross another wall, either by a high stile or through a broken gate on the left (Wp.5 30M) into the **Ariant** estate.

Maintaining direction (NNE), we climb through the rocks directly ahead of the stile, where there's a red waymark. Following occasional cairns and waymarks, and even more occasional stretches of clear path, we continue winding through the *carritx* and rocks (NE), and start descending through a <u>very</u> overgrown stretch - though given the prevailing invasion of *carritx*, it would be simpler to distinguish the 'undergrown' patches. If you haven't got a GPS, look for the cairns.

Rough walking, occasionally using our hands to lower ourselves between rocks, brings us down to what appears to be a natural descent off to the left. It may be natural, but it ain't for us.

We climb to the right, as indicated by blue and yellow waymarks on a large cairn-topped rock (Wp.6 45M), maintaining our general direction (NNE) for 50 metres before bearing left (NNW) up a rocky escarpment to a large cairn on a broad, flat rock. Continuing on the level, we pass above a shallow depression and another natural-not-for-us descent to the left.

Maintaining direction (ENE), we climb above the depression (Wp.7 55M) and briefly follow a very faint path before climbing steeply (NNE) up a rocky watershed to a yellow arrow, where we bear left onto a *coll* with clear views of the sea (Wp.8 60M).

... dramatic views en route ...

The way becomes slightly clearer as we descend to cross what must once have been a small lagoon and is now a *carritx* covered cirque. Winding through the *carritx*, we climb briefly before resuming our descent and coming into view of the **Rafal d'Ariant** plain.

After passing an old sign for 'Mortitx', we bear left and descend steeply, soon coming into view of the **Rafal d'Ariant** farmhouse. We then zigzag down below marvellously eroded cliffs to the house (Wp.9 90M).

There are at least four extensions possible from the farmhouse:

(1) peeking over the cliffs to the north (quite sickening if you suffer from vertigo);

(2) peering into the mouth of the **Cova de ses Buixes**, or **Witches' Cave**, which is the standard end to this walk;

(3) descending for a bathe (when the water's calm) at the **Caleta d'Ariant**; or

(4) in fine weather, exploring the **Torrent Fondo de Mortitx**, which is the start of the alternative return via the gorge.

For the first three, we take the clearly visible but occasionally overgrown path to the east of the house down to a small spring with an arched roof. After the spring, we head for the **Musclo de ses Cordes**, the massive cave-riddled bluff to the north-east, crossing two walls and the dry bed of the torrent.

(1) To peek over the cliffs (15M return from the house), we leave the path 100 metres after the torrent and bear left, crossing flat pathless land to the rock shelf where the torrent used to spill into a waterfall.

(2) For the cave and the cove, we stay on the path to cross a broad pass behind the **Musclo de ses Cordes**. The path descends a shallow gully of reddish-brown rocks, passing a large rock, walled-in as a makeshift shelter (easily missed on the descent).

Five metres before a massive overhanging rock with a partial wall (Wp.10 a little over fifteen minutes from the house), cairns mark a faint way across the rocks to the left, at the end of which (10M return from Wp.10) a shelf over a precipitous drop gives us a view of the entrance to the **Witches' Cave**.

(3) For the cove (15M return from Wp.10), we continue past the overhanging rock and follow the cairns for a very rough descent down to the *caleta*. Do not swim here if there's a swell. This extension is only for those who will do anything for a swim: it's a rough descent onto sharp volcanic rock that's murder on bare feet, though there's a nice ledge for rock bathing.

(4) To explore the **Torrent Fondo de Mortitx** and start the alternative return; take the rough path to the south-west of the house, passing a series of dead fig trees and running alongside a dry watercourse. Shortly after two large pine trees, we come to the torrent where there are various waymarks (Wp.11, 5M from the house). 100 metres to the right, under a tower of rock, a series of shallow pools lead up to one deep, permanent pool. Unfortunately, it's not really swimmable as access is difficult and the water's a bit scummy.

Either return the same way or take the…

Alternative return
Rafal d'Ariant is wild; the **Mortitx Gorge** is very, very wild and potentially very dangerous. There's no path, just lots of energetic scrambling. Only recommended for those who are happy without any sign of civilisation apart from intermittent cairns and waymarks. Do not venture into the gorge after rain or if there's a risk of rain. Do tell somebody where you're going.

Turning left at Wp.11 (0M), we follow the riverbed, hopping and scrambling from rock to rock. As we climb across a rock slope to the right of a first pool, the gorge starts to narrow and deepen.

After ten minutes, we come to a second pool, where we either have to get wet or gingerly edge our way across the shelving rock on the left. Less than two minutes after this second pool, we have a choice; our only one of the ascent so don't mess it up or you'll get into hellish difficulties further up! At an obvious fork in the gorge, we take the cairn and waymarked affluent to the left (Wp.12 12M).

Having made the correct choice, we hop from rock to rock up the affluent, absolved of responsibility for pathfinding – almost. After a particularly wild and narrow stretch where we have to constantly lever ourselves up with our hands between rocks, we come to a red waymark and yellow painted '30' mins (Wp.13 25M). Ignoring a rough path climbing towards a cave on the left, we carry straight on towards a cairn, after which a bilious green waymark indicates the onward route along the watercourse. The gorge gradually widens between towering rock pinnacles and we pass the occasional comforting cairn – it's not that you can get lost, but it's nice to know somebody's been here before you.

After an exhausting scramble, the gorge opens out into a natural sloping amphitheatre (40M). Following a faint path bearing right, we climb to the amphitheatre's southern 'gate', a massive rock with cliffs towering on either side (Wp.14 50M). To the left of the rock, a rough path and a final rocky stretch bring us to the base of a cliff, where we bear right on a clear path leading out of the gorge. Crossing a broken fence (60M), we stroll along a level dirt path that soon crosses a dry torrent, almost immediately after which we go through an olive grove to join the **l'Havanor** dirt track (Wp.15 65M). Turning left, we follow this track back past the **Mortitx** vineyard and farm buildings to the start of the walk (85M).

Puig de Sant Martí is the singular, slightly dull looking hillock behind **Playa Alcúdia**. Don't be deceived though. It's a stiff climb with some modest pathfinding problems, and the outlook on **Alcúdia**, the **Sa Pobla** plain, and the **Tramuntana** is splendid. If you're staying in **Alcúdia**, it's a must.

4*   1¾ -2H **   6.5 km   250m / 250m   0   ***

* Short Version 3 ** Short Version 1½h (estimated) *** in **Playa Alcúdia**

Short Version	Stroll
(More precisely, an easy version) in reverse, either to the smaller peak to the north, or on the easy, pathless route to the higher peak; in either case, return the same way.	To Wp.4 in reverse

Access: by car or on foot from **Playa Alcúdia**. From the **Playa Alcúdia** Tourism Information Office, we follow **Avenida Pere Mas I Reus** for 800 metres past the **Bellevue** complex to the **Edificio Siesta** apartments beside the bypass. The original start of the steep climb to the *puig* has been obliterated by the bypass, but if you trace an imaginary line up from the *avenida*, you should be able to pick out the bare earth of the watercourse we follow to the top.

Crossing the bypass (traffic is sparse but fast, so take care) we climb up the embankment just to the left of the crash barrier (Wp.1 0M) and scramble up a gap in the brush (marked with a small cairn) onto a mound of dirt. Bearing left towards a small stand of pine, we cross *carritx* and exposed rock to pick up the old path climbing to the right just before the pine. Ignoring a branch on the right, we climb towards the watercourse along a rough path studded with exposed rock and boulders. The path gets rougher and more overgrown the higher we go, obliging us to weave in and out of the watercourse, rapidly gaining height to emerge on the shallow *coll* to the left of the *puig* (Wp.2 25M).

To reach the summit, we bear right on a narrow 'way' winding along the ridge, passing two cairns and a pothole, before a pathless scramble over bare rock brings us to the northern tip of the *puig* (Wp.3 35M), in view of the telecommunication towers on the smaller peak to the north. From this little eyrie we have superb views through 360°.

There are two ways to descend, one quick and perilous along something approximating a path, the other more or less pathless but considerably less precipitous. Both end on the road to the telecommunication towers. Just below us, on the western side of the *puig*, is a short denuded spur with a few pine trees halfway along its back. We descend onto the upper part of this spur.

For the quick, perilous path
We bear slightly to the right on a rough path descending directly to the U-bend in the road (not for wet weather – at the best of times it's a crab-like descent and even the big rocks are unstable).

For the gentler, pathless route
We bear right <u>below</u> the limestone rocks capping the *puig* and follow the ridge to join the road 150 metres above the U-bend. Once on the road, we bear left and stroll down to a junction in front of a gated house (Wp.4 60M). Turning left, we follow a dirt track through the woods behind the *puig*, bearing left five minutes later at a Y-junction signposted 'Cova de Sant Martí'.

The dirt track climbs gently round the southern end of the *puig*, passing a cairn-marked path to the left (Wp.5 70M; for an alternative finish you can take this path, which curves round the hillside before dropping down to go through a tunnel under the bypass and emerge at Wp.7) and, 50 metres later, another track on the left.

Carrying straight on at the 'Canal d'en Bubo' T-junction (75M), we soon reach a gentle descent back to the bypass (Wp.6 80M).

Beyond the bypass, our track descends towards the lagoon, passing a large green metal cross marking the enclosed **Cova de Sant Martí** grotto.

Cova de Sant Martí

Twenty metres after the *cova*, we leave the track, bearing left on a narrow path winding through wild olive and pine woods till it's sandwiched between the bypass and a newly built slab of flats; if this path has been churned up by horse riders you can continue on the track to the metalled road. Ignoring a tunnel under the bypass (Wp.7 95M), we continue towards the **Edificio Siesta**, finally coming to a second tunnel, this time under the **Avenida Pere Mas I Reus**. The path continues toward the equestrian centre 200 metres further along, but we bear right to rejoin the *avenida*.

If doing this route in reverse
At the end of the **Avenida Pere Mas I Reus**, go to the left of the crash barriers between the by-pass junction and the **Edificio Siesta**, passing a white concrete bench and a small white building fronted with a ceramic map of Mallorca, just after which you'll find the path on your left.

The **Talaia d'Alcúdia** can be a bit of a motorway, especially on the dull, 'classic' route from the north, but it's popular with good reason, boasting excellent views, both inland and out to sea. It may seem a little perverse to drive to the end of the peninsula then walk inland, but there's method to this madness as it means we can climb to the top by the little used western ridge and (subject to the safety warning in the text) end our walk with a swim.

4	2H *	8 km	350m / 350m	↻	0

* + 50M for the extension	**Short Version/Stroll & Extension**
	Platja des Coll Baix - not for the fragile or very young given the hazardous rocks and currents. Don't attempt it in flip-flops, either. At the very least, stout walking sandals or trainers are required. Also an attractive destination for a bike excursion from **Alcúdia** (ask for hire details at the Tourist Information Office).

Access: by car, bike or on foot from **Alcúdia** (see Walk 12); start as per Walk 12 and continue to the end of the **Camí de la Muntanya**. Drivers stop in the large turning circle just below the **Coll Baix** chain, cyclists at the bike rack in the **Área Recreativa**.

From the car park/turning circle (Wp.1 0M), we walk back along the **Camí de la Muntanya** and, shortly after a chained track to the left, turn right for 'Coll de na Benet' (Wp.2 7M) on a track alongside the bed of a dry torrent. The track peters out 150 metres later and we cross the dry torrent to take a clear, cairn marked path climbing into a mixed wood of pine and wild olive trees.

After running alongside the torrent, the path dips down, re-crossing the torrent twice, continuing through dense *carritx* and increasingly infrequent trees. After a fourth crossing, we climb away from the torrent alongside the course of an affluent, winding round a couple of fallen pine. Cairns then lead us away from the affluent along a narrow path traversing the hillside before dipping down to cross the head of the main torrent. A brief climb brings us to the crossroads at **Coll de na Benet** (Wp.3 30M), where we turn right towards the **Talaia d'Alcúdia** which has been visible for the last ten minutes.

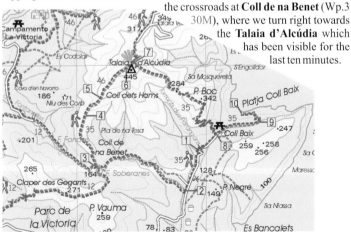

The Talaia from Coll Baix

At first we appear to be heading into pathless scrub, but after a few metres a faint trail (largely pioneered by goats but marked by man with cairns and the occasional red dot) becomes clear, winding through the *carritx* toward the **Talaia**, which is clearly visible for most of the ascent. A steady climb brings us to a small coll, after which the ascent becomes visibly steeper and the path dwindles to a cairn-marked way over bare rock (Wp.4 42M).

After an initial climb along the central spine, we follow a patch of path on the southern flank, at the end of which (Wp.5 44M), we clamber across the rocks back onto the central spine.

Zigzagging back and forth to break the gradient, but maintaining a northeasterly direction, we climb steeply to reach the foot of the summit crag (Wp.6 64M), where we can either scramble directly over the rocks onto the summit, or skirt left to join the main summit path just above a signpost indicating the descents to the *ermita* (on the left) and 'Coll Baix' (on the right) (Wp.7 71M).

Turning right, we follow a clear stony path round to the south of the **Talaia**. We then descend steadily to the watercourse between **Sa Mosquereta** and the **Torrent des Parangons**, after which a gentle climb skirts **Puig Boc**. A final steep descent, tamed by innumerable hairpin bends, brings us down to the **Coll Baix Área Recreativa** (Wp.8 120M), where we can either return directly to the car or turn left for **Platja des Coll Baix**.

Extension to Platja des Coll Baix + 50M

Not for the fragile or very young given the hazardous rocks and currents. Don't attempt it in flip-flops, either. At the very least, stout walking sandals or trainers are required. Turning left at Wp.8, we descend gently through a sickly pine wood, ignoring two branches to the left and passing a large V-trunked pine, immediately after which the path briefly divides. A third branch to the left is a shortcut, but we continue to a junction where fainter traces carry straight on and the main path turns sharp left (Wp.9 12M from Wp.8). Following the main path, we zigzag down through the trees, ignoring another shortcut near the end, 15 metres after which the path bears left on steps down to a red arrow indicating the 'way' over the rocks. We then pick our way along the rocks, keeping an eye on the alarmingly friable agglomerate to our left. It's evident from the debris that these cliffs regularly collapse, so don't venture along here after heavy rain. Following a roughly beaten path over the debris then hopping over the remaining rocks, we reach the beach (Wp.10 25M). We return by the same route.

WARNING: This beach is notoriously dangerous. The fact that the notice forbidding swimming in rough seas is in five languages is not merely the consequence of a casual polyglottism down the town hall. The undertow is strong, people drown. ONLY swim here when it's dead calm.

Puig d'Aguila is a firm favourite with holidaymakers, despite years of restricted access (no longer an issue), yet relatively few foreigners venture into the wilds around the more elevated summit of **La Mola**, doubtless largely because of those five little letters 'wilds'. There's nothing up there apart from us, the goats, and a lot of cairns - oh, and the views, of course, which are stunning.

There certainly aren't any paths for the most part, so it's pretty tough walking, but the frequent cairns are reassuring, and this might make a suitable excursion for a fit walker wanting to test themselves for the first time on rough, off-path terrain. It's very exposed, though, so don't go when it's hot and take plenty of water whatever the conditions.

Access: on foot from **Cala de San Vicenç**. The walk starts from the small circular car park behind **Cala Barques**, the most northerly of the four creeks that make up **Cala de San Vicenç**.

Short Version: in reverse via the main track to Wps. 22, 21, or 19 particularly recommended when the low lying evening sun illuminates the **Cavall Bernat** cliffs.

We start from the circular **Cala Barques** carpark in **Cala de San Vicenç** (Wp.1 0M). 100 metres up the **Avenguda de Cavall Bernat,** we turn right (Wp.2) on stairs climbing to a dirt track where we bear right again (Wp.3) to reach a gate and a monument commemorating the Republican POWs whose forced labour laid the track, which would be very laudable if the monument itself didn't look distressingly like a homemade barbecue (Wp.4 6M).

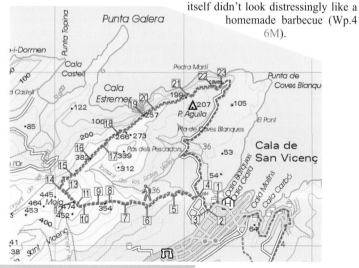

Going through the small pedestrian gate on the right, we immediately leave the track, turning left on a very faint path winding through the scrub parallel to the wall. **La Mola** is already visible directly ahead of us.

At first it seems as if we're going nowhere fast, but within 50 metres of the track, a red arrow painted on a rock indicates a cairn-marked route climbing half-right. Heading in a westerly direction and taking advantage of the patches of bare rock amid the *carritx* and dwarf palm, we climb steadily toward the back of the long sloping ridge on our right (which we follow for most of the ascent), where we pass a distinctive ball of rock, actually two fissured boulders sandwiched together (Wp.5 18M).

There are cairn-marked routes above and below here, but we favour the higher route to the right climbing onto the back of the ridge. Easy, off-path climbing brings us onto the first of two distinct rocky rises preceding the main ascent (Wp.6 32M).

The obvious way up would seem to be via the long shoulder off to our left, but as we traverse the second rise and cross a scruffy coll, it becomes clear that the main ascent is through the chaos of rock directly ahead of us, the start of which is indicated by cairns and large red waymarks (Wp.7 39M).

La Mola from near Wp.7

If you were of an uncommonly optimistic temperament, you might identify patches of trodden way here, but since they go every which way and have more to do with hoof than boot, stick with the cairn-marked route. After briefly disappearing from view, the summit comes into sight again as we cross a shallow pass (Wp.8 52M) and continue climbing to reach a coll between La Mola and a distinct rocky outcrop on our left. On the far side of the coll, cairns and a distant red waymark indicate the route for the final ascent (Wp.9 57M).

Climbing to the left of **La Mola**, we pass a solitary, rather sickly looking oleaster, bent back against the bare rock by an unequal battle with the elements (Wp.10 67M). After the tree, we climb straight up a stony gully, then bear right to reach a natural gateway in the rock (Wp.11 72M) just 50 metres short (50 fairly rough metres) of the summit, on the northern side of which you maybe blessed with a little shade (Wp.12 76M).

Our return route passes to the left of the large rocky outcrop visible to the northeast, but first we descend to the north, picking our way across rough ground densely carpeted with *carritx* and shrubs to a cluster of three cairns at the head of the gully that feeds the **Torrent de les Rotes Velles** (Wp.13 85M), from where we can see a line of large cairns along the rise defining the northern side of the gully.

Cala Castell

The walking becomes easier as we traverse more exposed rock to reach the cairn-marked rise, where fabulous views open out over **Punta Topina** and **Cala Castell** (Wp.14 88M).

Punta Galera

Bearing right, we descend along the cairn-marked route (NE), bringing into view the spectacular slender spit of **Punta Galera**.

Maintaining a north-easterly direction, we cross a distinct stony circle of reddish brown earth (Wp.15 96M) and aim for two humps of rock on a small ridge directly behind a cluster of pine trees clinging to the cliff tops. We cross the first hump (Wp.16 104M) then pass to the right of the second hump (Wp.17 108M), from where we descend half-right toward the remains of a wall below the large rocky outcrop seen from **La Mola**.

Crossing the wall via a faint trodden way (Wp.18 114M), we head for the obvious outstanding cliff top eyrie (NE), descending to a pronounced dip before climbing on what is now, to all intents and purposes, a path. After the eyrie (Wp.19 125M), the path disappears briefly and we descend across good, firm rock to recover a rough, intermittent path (Wp.20) that weaves across a small *carritx* covered plateau to a prominent conical cairn (Wp.21 136M), the hub for several cairn-marked routes.

The main **Aguila** summit topped with a flat trig point lies off to the right, but directly ahead of us (NE) we can see a small patch of orange spoil, marking the lower **Aguila** summit. Aiming for this, we descend on an initially invisible but soon clear path along the near side of the depression between the prominent cairn and the main summit. Skirting the small **Aguila** summit with its patch of spoil and the open mouth of an old shaft (Wp.22 142M), we follow a clear path zigzagging down to join the end of the dirt track (Wp.23 145M) for a gentle stroll back to the start.

Port de Sóller, **Sóller**, the **Mirador de Ses Barques** and **Cala Tuent** provide a set of local resources for us to enjoy a 'Great Day's Adventure' that combines hiking with scenic boat and tram rides to produce a unique multi-activity adventure.

Much of our itinerary features as the area's most popular guided walk and there is good reason for it to be popular. We can enjoy the route at our own pace and if it can seem crowded due to group excursions, we can be heartened by knowing that we are doing it for 'free'; well, the walking part is free though we still have to pay for our boat trip and tram fares.

| 4 | 4½ H | 16 km | | 550m 550m | * | 3-4 |

* linear one-way walk, with a boat trip back to Sóller

From **Sóller**, we follow Walk 7 (Wps. 1-5, see pages 29 & 30) then Walk 16 (Wps. 7-5 in reverse, now 6,7 & 8 in Walk 37, see page 49 then 48) for a stonking hike up to the **Mirador de Ses Barques**. Allow 90 minutes for the 300+ metre ascent.

Balitx de Dalt

From the *mirador*, we continue on Walk 42 traversing the **Balitx Valley** to the **Coll de Biniamar** (Wps. 1-10 Walk 41, 8-17 Walk 37, 103 minutes, pages 108 & 109), where we follow the wayposted itinerary over the coll.

Balitx d'Avall farmhouse

Two hundred metres later, we join Walk 21 at Wp.7, page 59 then page 58). We then follow Walk 21 to its start above **Cala Tuent** (Wps. 7-1 Walk 21, Wps. 18-22 Walk 37, 80 minutes), from where we make our way down to the quay to await the arrival of the Barcos Azules boat at 16.50.

Our scenic boat ride to **Port de Sóller** will see us arriving at approximately 17.40. Thereafter, a short stroll takes us to the tram terminus for a rattling good ride back to the centre of **Sóller**.

Great views on route -

While we are using parts of the route descriptions from Walk 7, Walk 16, Walk 42 and Walk 21, we've created a single GPS waypoint file for our Great Day Out.

Key points in planning our Great Day Out are:-

You must pre-book the Barcos Azules 'taxi boat', 15€ single fare. The service is seasonal so check with both the Barcos Azules website http://www.barcosazules.com/pagina .php?Cat=3 - and at **Port de Sóller** before finalising your plans. Barcos Azules can be contacted by phone at 971 63 01 70.

Walking times on our routes total four

and a half hours. Add twenty minutes at each end (to reach the start of Walk 7 and find our way down to the landing point in **Cala Tuent**) and that means we should leave **Sóller** by 11.30.

Depending on personal preference, also allow time for breaks (coffee and cake at the **Mirador de Ses Barques** are most welcome after the big climb, as is orange juice at the **Balitx d'Avall** farmhouse, and probably a picnic, too), breathers, photo opportunities, and simply standing still staring at the views, in which case we should probably set off at about 10.30.

- and yet more great views

If you don't feel like the big climb out of **Sóller** at the start, the **Mirador** can also be reached via bus 354 (seasonal service). The bus leaves **Port de Sóller** (**Calle 11 de Maig**) at 9am and **Sóller** (**Calle Cetre**) at 9.10, and runs from Monday to Saturday.

Alternatively, the very energetic could make their Big Day Out bigger still, by taking one of the following diversions off the main route:

Nº1
Walk 42 Waypoints 10-12 (+ 45M return + 1.6km return + 170 metres climbing) to the **Torre de na Seca** martello tower, offers wild walking and some of the finest views on the island.

Nº2
Walk 21 Waypoints 7-8 (+ 40M return + 1.2km return + 50 metres climbing) enjoys views that are more readily accessible and only marginally less sublime from the superbly situated house at **Sa Costera**.

Nº3
Walk 21 Waypoints 4-6 (+40M return + 1km return + 150 metres climbing) gives us the opportunity to take a dip in splendid isolation at the **Fábrica de Luz**, an abandoned hydroelectric generating station.

Remember if taking one or more of these diversions that the boat leaves **Cala Tuent** at 16.50, it does not wait, even if you have a ticket.

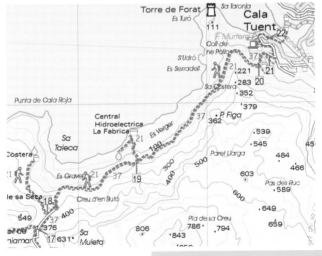

38 PUIGPUNYENT: GALATZÓ from the SOUTH

The most distinctive summit in the west, **Galatzó** is conventionally approached from the north via the **Pas des Cossis** and the **Boal de ses Serveres Área Recreativa**. Unfortunately, this route suffered serious damage during the forest fires of 2013, so while we are waiting for the vegetation to recover, we must 'make do' with this short ascent from the south. I put 'make do' in inverted commas because, despite the diminutive little squiggle representing the itinerary on the map, this is a very fine little walk indeed, and involves a strenuous ascent on rough ground that should not be undertaken lightly.

| 5 | 2H 35M | 8 km | ⛰ | 550m / 550m | out & back | 🍴 0 |

Access: by car

To reach the start, from km 11.1 of the PMV1032 (100 metres west of **Puigpunyent** church, Wp.1) take the **Camí de sa Teulera** north, more obviously signposted 'La Reserva', setting the odometer at zero. Follow the signs for 'La Reserva' to a triple junction at km 3.2 in front of a house called **Es Cucui** (Wp.2). The **La Reserva** route descends to the left here, but we stay on the main lane, passing a quarry at km 4.2 (Wp.3). Park at km 4.7 at the bottom of a dirt track forking right. N.B. if there's no room here, stay on the lane and turn right at km 5 on a steep, narrow lane leading to Wp.5.

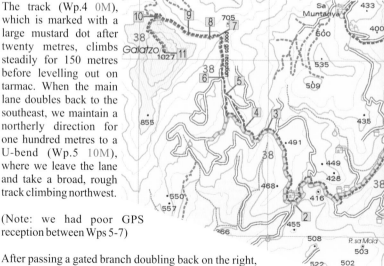

The track (Wp.4 0M), which is marked with a large mustard dot after twenty metres, climbs steadily for 150 metres before levelling out on tarmac. When the main lane doubles back to the southeast, we maintain a northerly direction for one hundred metres to a U-bend (Wp.5 10M), where we leave the lane and take a broad, rough track climbing northwest.

(Note: we had poor GPS reception between Wps 5-7)

After passing a gated branch doubling back on the right, we bear sharp right at a Y-junction and climb a stony trail, at the end of which a waypost and waymarking arrows mark the start of a narrow path (Wp.6 15M).

The path soon broadens to a trail, climbing steadily through woodland badly

El Bisbe from the south

battered by storm damage. The woods thin out as we pass the path to the firewatch tower on **Coll des Carniceret** (Wp.7 25M), after which fine views open out along the eastern ridge of **Es Puntals**, **Planicia** and beyond them, the high **Tramuntana**. We continue our steady climb to the west on a clear path winding through *carritx*, *madroño* and small oak.

There are at least two parallel paths here, but all converge at a waypost on a rocky shoulder (Wp.8 35M), from where we can see a grassy slope to the north of the main summit with what appears to be a cross silhouetted against the skyline.

Looking towards Estellencs

Aiming for the 'cross' (in fact a signpost), we follow a narrow but clear path along the northeastern flank of the mountain. The path descends slightly to cross a spill of large boulders (Wp.9 45M), which are reasonably stable but still require some care. We now have a long, steady climb passing below the distinctive pillar of **El Bisbe** (The Bishop) to the 'cross' signpost next to the foundations of a small hut (Wp.10 55M).

Bearing left (SW), we climb a rough, stony path behind the foundations of the hut then, after following a clear stretch of path for 75 metres, bear left up a watercourse.

At the top of the watercourse, we continue climbing steadily, maintaining a southerly direction to reach the waymarked foot of the last 50 metre scramble up to the trig point on the summit (Wp.11 85M). We return via the same route.

The **Fita del Ram** is the highest point on the heavily wooded massif between **Esporles** and **Puigpunyent**, an area that was once a vital source of charcoal, as a result of which the mountain is crisscrossed with charcoal burners' paths and speckled with hundreds of *sitjes*.

There are several ways up the **Fita del Ram** (*fita* means landmark, Ram, literally 'bunch' or 'bouquet', was the name of the family who owned the land in the eighteenth century), but in this instance we stick to the best known and consequently best waymarked route via the **Ermita de Maristel**.

I say 'best known', yet the itinerary rarely features in guidebooks, which is baffling as this lovely woodland walk should be on every walker's must-do list. You've got to like getting away from it all, though; the top's not very wild, but it is very isolated. Pathfinding near the end requires a certain amount of concentration, but is not dauntingly complex.

*   but allow 5 hours

Access: on foot from **Esporles**. Motorists can cut fifty minutes from the full itinerary by driving to the **Son Ferra** estate (turn left for 'Es Verger / Área Recreativa Son Tries' as you arrive in **Esporles** from the south, immediately setting the odometer at zero; the narrow gate at Wp.7 is at km 2.3), though I don't particularly recommend this, as the path out of **Esporles** is an attractive one in its own right.

For the full itinerary, we also take the **Es Verger** road (Wp.1 0M), but turn left at the first crossroads. Carrying straight on at the next crossroads (no nameplate, though we're following **Carrer des Quarter**), we pass the *Guardia Civil* barracks, then turn right at the next junction (onto **Carrer des Rafal**), passing houses N°s 17 & 19. When the road swings left and descends back towards the PM104, we maintain direction on a narrow track between stone walls (Wp.2 6M).

The track climbs through a cluster of houses, crossing a small rise, after which we turn right (Wp.3 10M) behind an old house half painted white. We go through a wicker and wire gate, then follow a pleasant terrace path curving round to a T-junction (Wp.4 15M), where we again turn right on a path climbing alongside the narrow, partially tailored channel of a *torrent*.

After a second wicker and wire gate, we join a dirt track (Wp.5 20M) which we follow back to the **Es Verger** road. Forty metres up the road (Wp.6) we turn left on a narrow, overgrown, roughly paved path, climbing between fenced walls and a host of hedgerow flowers to a surfaced track just below the **Es Verger** road. On the far side of the road is a small gate, behind which a large carob tree overshadows the *ermita* path (Wp.7 30M).

The main gate is locked, but a narrow one-person-wide entrance lets us

squeeze through onto the path, our route confirmed by a hand-painted 'ERMITA' sign shortly after the carob tree.

The path almost immediately joins a narrow track climbing to the right of the **Son Ferra** farmhouse (Wp.8), behind which we go through (and shut!) a gate.

Son Ferra at Wp.8

Climbing into the woods, the track runs parallel to then crosses an old trail, immediately after which we go through another gate. The track, which is mainly concreted here, climbs steeply through the woods. At a second gap in the concrete there is a small, very flimsily fenced *mirador* off to the right (Wp.9 45M).

After the next and final stretch of concrete ends, the gradient eases then levels off altogether, passing two faint charcoal-burners' paths off to the left. We then climb gently (N) to a sharp left-hand bend, where a broad trail branches right (Wp.10 62M) leading in one hundred metres to the **El Cor de Jesús** statue/*mirador* (Wp.11) overlooking **Esporles**.

Returning to Wp.10 (72M), we continue up the track for less than 100 metres to a clear, cairn-marked shortcut (Wp.12) joining one of the paths passed after the end of the concrete.

El Cor de Jesús at Wp.11

Ermita de Maristel

Turning right, we follow this path, crossing a wall and passing a cave, before rejoining the track just below the **Ermita de Maristel** (Wp.13 83M). The *ermita* dates from 1888 and is of no great architectural interest, but the superb location confirms once again that the rewards of a religious vocation are worldly as well as heavenly.

On the far side of the grassy clearing to the south of the *ermita*, we go through a gap in a wall and follow a cairn-marked trail to the right alongside another wall. The trail meanders through the woods, crossing the end of another broad trail between two *sitjes* (Wp.14), at which point the cairns guide us onto a narrow path winding between low outcrops of rock.

Passing a tiny, mossy *aljub* and crossing a wall (Wp.15 94M), we come to a second clearing where a small cabin is currently being restored.

At the end of the clearing, we climb back into the woods, bearing right to cross a wall (Wp.16), after which the trail levels off in a particularly delightful area of woodland where the oak and strawberry trees are more evenly intermingled.

Seventy-five metres after a lime-kiln, we ignore a minor branch on the left (Wp.17) and continue on the main trail, passing a grassy roofed reservoir (Wp.18 102M), beyond which we ignore a turning to the right and climb through a chicane before resuming our pleasant, level stroll.

We stick to the main trail (if you happen to see cairns on the left next to a rock marked with a red cross, ignore them) until it climbs to a breach in a wall (Wp.19 110M). Immediately after crossing the wall, we leave the main trail which descends SW, and turn left (SE) as indicated by cairns and faint waymarks. There are long stretches of reasonably clear path here, but it often disappears in bare rock, so it's important to follow the cairn-marked route for the rest of the climb.

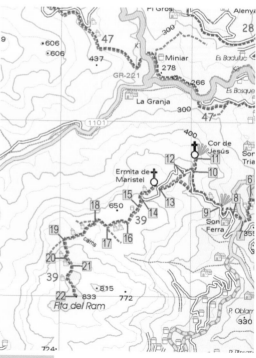

In a further seventy-five metres, the cairns lead us through a natural passage between two large outcrops of rocks, after which we continue climbing parallel to the wall crossed at Wp.19.

A little under 100 metres after the natural passage, we veer away from the wall (SSW), and continue our steady climb to a *sitja* (Wp.20 122M).

Red waymarks appear to mark a route off to the right, but we stay with the cairns, climbing to the left of the *sitja* (W) on a relatively clear path, passing twin *sitjes* fifty metres later.

Behind the twin *sitjes* are what appear to be the rocks of the summit. They ain't! After going up a rocky way to the north of the false summit, we climb behind it, crossing a tumbledown wall (Wp.21 127M) linking it with another large outcrop, again not the summit.

Galatzó as seen from the summit

A *sitja* beyond the wall marks the start of another reasonably clear path (SW), passing a second *sitja* and bisecting a third, 150 metres after which a narrow chute blocked with natural steps leads to the trig-point on the summit (Wp.22 138M).

'Summit' is a somewhat grand term for a tiny hump of rock just poking over the treetops, but whatever you call it, it's one of those places you won't regret visiting. The views are predictably superb, stretching from **Massanella** in the east to **Galatzó** in the west, but more beguiling still is the immediate landscape, a magical, peaceful tangle of twisty-trunked oaks rimed with hanks of lichen, the occasional ghostly shadow of an unseen seagull gliding overhead, the only sound being bird song, the hum of insects, and the occasional patter of a falling leaf.

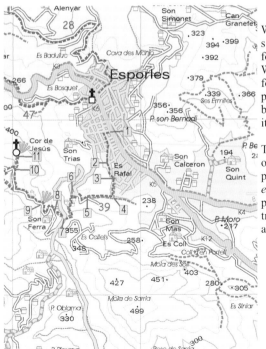

We descend almost by the same route, carefully following the cairns back to Wp.19 and, after Wp.15, forking left on the narrower path rather than taking the broad trail that presents itself straight ahead.

The only difference is that, once on the shortcut path passing the cave below the *ermita*, we stay on the main path to emerge on the dirt track below rather than above Wp.10.

In 1867 the Austrian Archduke Ludwig Salvator visited Mallorca and liked it so much he stayed, establishing a tradition that has continued to the present day. Ludwig, however, was more ambitious than modern migrants. His season in the sun was conceived on a large scale and instead of toiling along charcoal-burners' paths, he set about improving the **Teix** massif, laying a bridleway complete with refuges and *miradors*, a rich man's folly for which generations of walkers have been grateful.

Previously I have broken the itinerary in two, a short walk to the **Mirador de ses Puntes** via the **Coll de s'Estret** (AKA **Coll de son Gallard**) and a longer excursion climbing via **Fontanelles** before descending directly from the **Coll de s'Estret**. Using Walk 49 Wps.1-7 this is still possible, in the first instance providing a 7km, two hour walk with an exertion rating of three, climbing 400 metres, in the second a three hour, 10km walk with the same exertion rating and a climb of 500 metres. The two itineraries are complementary, but if time is short, the full loop is highly recommended. There is a very slight risk of vertigo between Wps.7 & 8. If vertigo is a serious problem, best opt for the short version via **Coll de s'Estret**.

5 | 3H 25M | 13.3 km | 650m / 650m | ⟳ | ⚠ | 🍴 0

Access: on foot from **Valldemossa**. From the fountain car-park on the main road through **Valldemossa**, take **Carrer de la Venerable Sor Aina** towards the cemetery and football pitch, then second right onto **Carrer de Joan Fuster**, and first left onto **Carrer de Oliveres**, at the end of which a broad walking trail (part of the **GR221**) begins beside the gates of the **Son Gual Petit** *finca*. If arriving by car, park at the end of **Carrer de Oliveres**.

We take the **GR221** trail (Wp.1 0M), which shadows the **Son Gual** driveway before swinging left and climbing to approach a stile, just before which, we leave the GR and turn sharp right on a broad charcoal burners' trail supported by a low retaining wall (Wp.2 13M). The trail climbs steadily, then levels out and goes

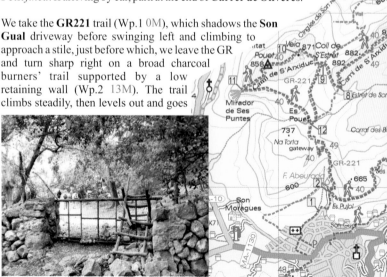

The stile just after Wp.2

through a wall gateway, from where it winds round a broad wooded valley. It then climbs again, becoming a little overgrown, before swinging left at a distinctive, triple-trunked pine for a steep to steady climb ending at a *sitja* and ruined shelter (Wp.3 53M).

Leaving the *sitja* on our right, we carry straight on (NW) for 10 metres to pick up a cairn and waymarked route climbing over the rocks to the north to reach an oak wooded ridge. Sticking to the cairn marked route, we climb (NE) over two outcrops of rock to emerge on the rough limestone plateau below the scattered **Fontanelles** summits. Taking care to follow the cairns, we cross the plateau in a northerly direction to reach a minor branch of the **Archduke's Path** (Wp.4 68M). Bearing right, we climb a gentle slope to join the main **Archduke's Path** (Wp.5 78M). Turning left, we climb past **Puig Caragoli** (Wp.6 83M) and rejoin the GR beside two cairns, indicating the GR's descent to **Deià** (Wp.7 86M).
\

The vertiginous stretch

Carrying straight on, we continue on what is probably the most spectacular and vertiginous stretch of the **Archduke's Path**, enjoying fabulous views (notably of **Sa Foradada**, Walk 15) before zigzagging down through woodland for five minutes to reach a signposted branch on the right (Wp.8 118M).

Leaving the main path, we turn right and descend to **Coll de s'Estret** where there is a long V-shaped bench (Wp.9 128M), at which point those who opted for the shorter, non-vertiginous version will join the full itinerary.

Carrying straight on (turning left if you've just climbed from **Es Pouet**), we climb once again to reach the refuge on **Puig Veia** (Wp.10 143M). Following the cobbled bridleway, we pass the **Pover** trig point and a natural mirador overlooking the coast before descending to the **Mirador de ses Puntes** (Wp.11 158M), from where there are tremendous views across the Valldemossa plain towards **Galatzó** (Walk 38) and, predictably enough, an equally tremendous drop. Five metres behind the *mirador*, the bridleway bears east for a gentle, shady stroll back to rejoin the GR at the **Es Pouet** well (Wp.12 173M), where we turn right to descend along a beautifully graded trail winding through sun-dappled woodland back to Wp.2.

41 TEIX FROM VALLDEMOSSA

Teix is one of Mallorca's most popular summits and the ascent can be a bit of a motorway, as a result of which several classic routes have been closed off by disgruntled landowners. Nowadays, the majority of walkers approach via the **Archduke's Path**, following Walk 49 to Wp.9 before descending to join Wp.20 of the present itinerary and climbing from there. However, for those of you who like getting off the beaten track, I strongly recommend the little known approach via the **Serra des Cairats**. For my money, it's one of the most spectacular walks in Mallorca. The only drawback is that pathfinding is challenging. If you're not using a GPS, you need to study the text carefully for Wps.7-14.

N.B. The **Serra des Cairats** is called **Serra de Son Moragues** on some maps.

Access on foot: from the playground at the eastern end of **Valldemossa**, follow the MA1110 toward **Palma** for 100 metres then climb the stairs on the left just before the bottle bank. Turn right to pass the house with the castellated tower and follow **Carrer Lluis Vives** into **Carrer Xesc Forteza**. 100 metres after a carob tree on an island in the road, bear left on a narrow dirt track signposted '*Refugi*' (Wp.1 0M).

Short Version
Turn left at Wp.16 to rejoin the main route at Wp.21. 2h30, same exertion rating.

Access by car: follow the MA1110 toward **Palma** then take the first turning on the left, signposted 'Urbanizacion s'Arxiduc / Refugi Son Moragues'. The *urbanizacion* road climbs to the left to pass a large house (Nº20) with imposing black gates.

The walk starts on the track (Wp.1 0M) branching off to the right just before this house.

200 metres from the road, the track goes through new gates. We stay on

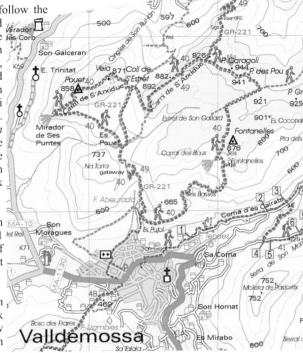

the main track for a little over a kilometre, ignoring minor branches to left and right accessing terraces. After a second new gate and a cattle grid, we bear left into the **Cairats Valley** (Wp.2 15M). 200 metres later, we leave the main track and double back to the right on a minor track zigzagging up in a southwesterly direction (Wp.3 19M).

Ignoring a minor divergence to the right, we climb to a T-junction (Wp.4 30M), where we turn left then fork right 50 metres later (Wp.5) on a cairn-marked shortcut across a bend in the track. After we rejoin it, the track dwindles to a trail shadowing a terracing wall, at the end of which it divides into two narrow paths (Wp.6 41M). We take the cairn-marked path climbing to the right, then turn left at a T-junction 25 metres later (Wp.7). 50 metres after that, we fork left at a Y-junction (Wp.8), passing a *sitja* after another 50 metres. We then cross a second *sitja* (Wp.9) and bear right, following the path as it traverses the slope, passing a metal 'Caça Controlada' sign (Wp.10 52M).

Keeping an eye out for successive cairns, we cross two distinct bands of rock, beyond which we reach the foot of a steep, gully-like pass (Wp.11 56M). A brief but strenuous scramble, occasionally hands on and generally ankle deep in leaf mulch (beware of dislodging

Wp.11 - the pass

loose stones if there are other people behind you), brings us to the top of the pass where there is a third *sitja* (Wp.12 63M).

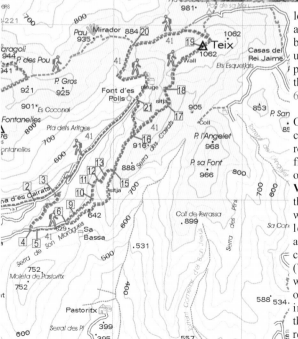

Our path then climbs through the rocks to the right, fine views opening out over **Valldemossa** and the mountains to the west. The path levels off as it approaches concentric *sitjes* (Wp.13 69M), after which a cairn up to our right (Wp.14) indicates a way through the rocks to reach twin *sitjes*, above which we join a broad trail (Wp.15 74M).Turning left, we take a well-earned breather as we stroll along the broad trail to join the **Serra des Cairats** trail (AKA **Camí des Caragol**) at a U-bend (Wp.16 81M).

descending to the font - short version

For the short version rejoining the main track at **Font des Polls**, turn left to enjoy an easy descent along a lovely snaking trail that reaches Wp.21 in a little over 10 minutes.

For Teix, turn right, climbing steadily until the trail ends at the last *sitja* (Wp.17 96M), where a rough stony way dotted with cairns and red waymarks climbs (E) to a wall topped with a fence.

Bearing left, we follow the wall for 50 metres before crossing it by a second waymarked breach (Wp.18 112M). Thereafter, frequent cairns and waymarks guide us up a steep, but relatively easy climb across the rocks (NE) to a gap in the wall girdling the southern side of the **Teix**, from where a gentler climb leads to the trig point on the summit (Wp.19 132M).

To return to the **Cairats Valley**, we descend (ENE) to the coll between **Teix** and its sister peak, where we bear left (NNW) down to the **Pla de sa Serp** plateau. Following the broad, obvious trail (WNW) we cross a slight rise to a Y-junction just before a wall. The two branches rejoin beyond the wall for a final rocky descent to a large pile of stones on the **Archduke's Path** (Wp.20 147M).

a limekiln in the Cairats valley

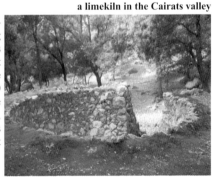

Bearing left, we follow a well-stabilized path zigzagging down to the **Son Moragues** refuge, where the broad dirt track descending into the **Cairats Valley** begins. 200 metres later, we come to the **Font des Polls** picnic area, where the short version joins the main itinerary from the left (Wp.21 172M).

From here, we simply follow the track down, down, down to return to the start, a descent that is very straightforward and initially very hard on the knees until the gradient eases and we leave the **Son Moragues Área Recreativa** via a stone-stepped stile. 200 metres after the stile, a waymarked shortcut slices across a final S-bend just short of Wp.3.

The linear route between the **Mirador de ses Barques** and **Cala Tuent** returning by boat is a classic and can be a bit crowded, but like most popular things it is popular for a reason, in this instance lovely trails, great views, and (no small consideration in Mallorca) farmhouses that actually welcome walkers. This variant features the first part of the standard itinerary exploring the **Balitx Valley** before branching off the beaten track to visit an old watchtower that enjoys some of the finest views on the island.

If you want to do the standard one way route, see Walk 37 for details of access and planning.

Access: via car or bus (L354 seasonal service from **Sóller** and **Port de Sóller**), or on foot from **Sóller** (see A Great Day Out on P.97). The walk starts from the **Mirador de ses Barques** at km45 of the MA10.

From the **Mirador de ses Barques** carpark, we take the stepped path signposted 'Cala Tuent, Sa Costera, Balitx' (Wp.1 0M). Until Wp.10 the walk is clearly wayposted, so the book can be stowed after a preliminary perusal. Given that the linear route to **Cala Tuent** is very, very popular with organized hiking groups, it's best to set out early or late to avoid the crowds.

the cobbled trail

After a brief climb along a charming cobbled trail (the **Camí Vell de Balitx**), we emerge on a concrete track in front of a small house (Wp.2 5M), where we bear left. Going through a gateway, we descend across olive terraces to join the main **Balitx** dirt track, where we bear right (Wp.3 18M) and stroll alongside the immaculately tended fields of the **Balitx de Dalt** (Upper Balitx) estate, beyond which we can see the **Torre de na Seca** on the far side of the valley.

200 metres after going through a gateway in front of the **Balitx de Dalt** farmhouse, the main track doubles back to the left and a branch forks off to the right, between which we carry straight on along the cobbled *camí vell* (Wp.4 43M). The trail passes two springs before rejoining the main track beside the ruin of **Balitx d'en Mig** (in the middle) (Wp.5 50M). Continuing on the track, we descend into the spectacular trough of the **Balitx** valley. 100 metres above a small house, we leave the track, descending slightly to the left to recover the *camí vell*, signposted 'Balitx d'Avall, Tuent' (Wp.6 63M). After a steady descent, we rejoin the main track (Wp.7 76M) just above the **Balitx d'Avall**

(lower) farmhouse famous for its orange juice, which, given the location, is very reasonably priced at 2 euros a glass. If the courtyard's not packed with a guided hiking party, it's well worth stopping for a glass and to inspect the collection of farm implements in the bar area. The people are friendly, too, despite living on a route that can, at its busiest, resemble a motorway.

Crossing the torrent below the farm, we leave the track again, turning right at a signposted junction (Wp.8 82M) to recover the cobbled *camí vell* as it zigzags up the wooded terraces of the valley's northeastern flank. After a steady slog, we rejoin the now very rough track (Wp.9 97M) for the final climb toward the **Coll de Biniamar**. At the last bend immediately below the coll, we leave the crowds behind and turn left (Wp.10 103M) on a broad trail behind a waypost indicating that the standard route continues over the coll. Heading west, we follow a contour, passing some wonderful rock formations while superb views of the **Balitx** valley open out behind us. After going through a gate, we climb to a turning circle at the end of the trail, where cairns and green waymarks indicate the steep climb onto the ridge (Wp.11 112M).

This stretch is off-path, but though there's abundant *carritx* and the *torre* isn't visible until the last moment, pathfinding is not a problem. The way becomes clearer, and possibly a little steeper toward the top, but don't despair because the views from the *torre* (Wp.12 127M) would justify double the effort.

view from the torre

We return via the same route with the option of following the track at Wps.9, 7, 5, & 3 for a moderately easier gradient, and maybe even a lift if you're lucky!

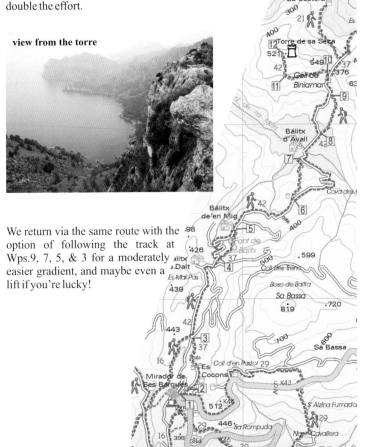

Our second itinerary based on the pleasant pastoral valley of **Orient** is a challenging circuit, climbing to a wonderful natural *mirador* on the **Talaia de Cals Reis** before looping through two exceptional passes. There's a gruelling climb halfway round and pathfinding is problematic between Wps.16 & 17, but otherwise pure pleasure, the highlights of the **Pas de s'Escaleta** and **Pas de s'Estaló** framing fabulous views and lovely woodland.

Short Version: to the **Talaia de Cals Reis** *mirador*, returning via the same route.

Access: on foot from **Orient**. There is a taxi-bus service to **Orient** from **Bunyola** (which can be reached by train and bus) bookable a day in advance on 617 365 365. If arriving by the taxi-bus, bear in mind, 3h20 is a 'pure' time. You should allow at least five hours for the full walk. Motorists should park in the main car park south of **Orient**.

From the bus stop/parking area immediately south of **Orient** (Wp.1 0M), we walk up the road for 275 metres toward the **Hermitage Hotel** and **Alaró** , then turn right in front of a large reservoir (Wp.2 4M) to go through a red gate into an orchard, where we bear left on a dirt track climbing (SW) to the oak forested slopes on the southern flank of the valley. After going through a gate into the woods, we turn left (Wp.3 9M) and follow a charcoal burners' trail climbing along the edge of the woods.

Ignoring a minor branch on the right (Wp.4 17M), we go through a gap in a wall, after which the trail levels off, following a terrace in an easterly direction before climbing briefly to the crest of a slight rise, where cairns on our right indicate the linear ascent of the **Talaia de Cals Reis** (Wp.5 22M).

At first, the **Talaia** branch is faint, but the way soon becomes a broad, rough trail that in turn dwindles to a narrow path (Wp.6 31M), 40 metres along which we enter a denser stand of oak.

Orient from the mirador

A steep climb brings us to a wall (Wp.7 39M), where we turn right and head north for 75 metres to a rocky platform that serves as a natural *mirador*, with superb views over the **Orient** valley and a large stretch of the **Tramuntana** (Wp.8 41M).

There is an off-path route continuing to the west from here marked with the very occasional cairn, but it is indiscernible and indescribable (we got to within 300 metres of Wp.20 before giving it up as a bad job), so I recommend returning to Wp.5 (54M) by the same route.

Heading east on the main path, we fork right at a Y-junction 150 metres after the **Talaia** turn-off (Wp.9) and follow a narrow path descending through lovely, fairytale woodland to the **Pas de s'Escaleta** (Wp.10 64M), a runoff channel carved into a rocky declivity, where a small wall has been built, inset with steps to aid the descent

Pas de s'Escaleta

Beyond the *pas* a good path zigzags down to join a concrete track, where we turn right (Wp.11 73M). We follow this track for the best part of two kilometres, initially descending steeply through a series of zigzags, then on an easier gradient shadowing the **Torrent de s'Estret**, enjoying the easy walking and picturesque scenery - very picturesque, look out for the Indian guru with a Great Dane!

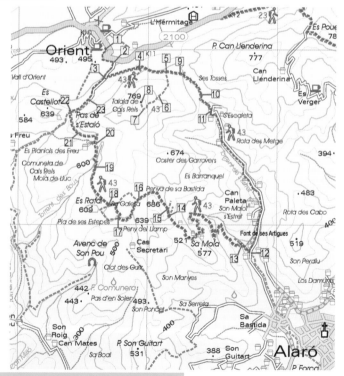

Eventually, we reach the covered and locked **Font de ses Artigues** and the cluster of houses of the same name. Immediately after the font, we turn right, stepping over a low, broken wall beside a locked gate (Wp.12 103M) then bearing left 75 metres later on a dirt track (Wp.13) that climbs very steeply across abandoned terraces.

This is the toughest stretch of the walk, so take your time and stop occasionally to enjoy the view over the **Estret** valley behind you, because the track of itself isn't terribly beguiling.

The track levels off briefly toward the top, but the punishing climb soon resumes, passing a succession of cabins and curving round below the streaked cliffs of the **Mola de sa Bastida** to approach the spine-like outcrop of **Sa Galera**.

Eventually, after what seems like forever, we pass two forks off to the right within 100 metres of each other (Wp.14 144M & Wp.15) and, 200 metres later, go through a gate (or by pass it to the right if it's locked), whereupon we relax, as the really hard work is done, though some care is required for pathfinding in the next fifteen minutes. Ignoring a branch off to the right 225 metres after the gate (Wp.16 153M), we stay on the main track till it reaches the entrance of the **Es Rafal** ruin (Wp.17 157M). Bearing right, we follow the track to the north for 150 metres, then west for 75 metres to go through a gap in a wall directly behind the ruin. Turning right on the far side of the wall (Wp.18), we follow a faint way running alongside the wall, at the end of which a cairn confirms that we are on trail.

The end of the walk is pure pleasure as we stroll along a narrow path well-marked with cairns, weaving our way through dense woodland and passing the head of the **Torrent des Bous** (Wp.19 169M). The path then climbs across exposed rock and goes through a gap in a wall (Wp.20 174M), after which a steady descent takes us past a miniature reservoir.

Following a contour, we cross a sheet of exposed rock (Wp.21 179M), 250metres after which we join the broad trail crossing the **Pas de s'Estaló** (Wp.22 183M).

Turning right then left 350 metres later (Wp.23), we rejoin our outward route at Wp.3.

Pas de s'Estalo

Puig Tomir is not the most distinctive of Mallorca's summits, but does enjoy a unique perspective on **Pollença** and the **Formentor** peninsula. More importantly, the way up is a glorious, rough little climb with a distinctly Pyrenean feel to it. Add to that a leisurely descent and long loop through remote countryside, and you've got an offer you can't refuse.

Puig Tomir

Don't be deceived by the brevity of the ascent, though. Although easy, it is a steep climb on rough ground and should not be undertaken by unaccompanied inexperienced walkers. Long trousers preferable between Wps.11 & 13.

5 | 4¼-5H | 13 km | 650m / 650m | ○ | 0

Access: by car or (starting from **Lluc**) bus (L330 from **Palma**, L354 from **Alcúdia**, **Pollença**, & Soller, L355 from **Alcúdia** and **Pollença**)

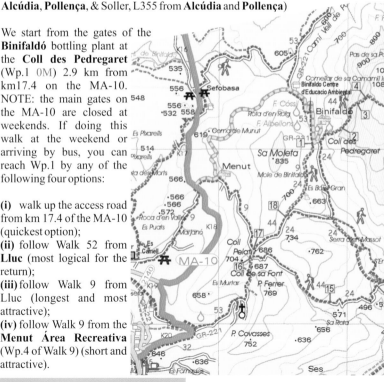

We start from the gates of the **Binifaldó** bottling plant at the **Coll des Pedregaret** (Wp.1 0M) 2.9 km from km17.4 on the MA-10. NOTE: the main gates on the MA-10 are closed at weekends. If doing this walk at the weekend or arriving by bus, you can reach Wp.1 by any of the following four options:

(i) walk up the access road from km 17.4 of the MA-10 (quickest option);
(ii) follow Walk 52 from **Lluc** (most logical for the return);
(iii) follow Walk 9 from Lluc (longest and most attractive);
(iv) follow Walk 9 from the **Menut Área Recreativa** (Wp.4 of Walk 9) (short and attractive).

Taking the path to the right of the bottling plant gates, we climb alongside the fence before bearing right for a steeper climb through the woods, following cairns and red waymarks. Above the woods, we cross a scree-filled gully (Wp.2 15M) and descend briefly before climbing to traverse the head of a broader scree slope. At the north-eastern tip of the scree slope, we bear right up a second narrow gully, passing a steel cable set in the rock as a handrail, and emerging midway along another scree-filled gully (Wp3 30M).

After climbing straight up this third gully, we scramble up a 5 metre high rockface (Wp.4 40M) with the help of two metal hoops and another steel cable - if this sounds alarming, bear in mind it has been tested in accordance with The Old English Sheepdog Trial (see Walk 8). We then follow a long curving valley for 50 metres before bearing right on a cairn-marked path climbing to a clear breach in the rock defining the valley.

classic rockscape below Puig Tomir

After the breach, we continue climbing (SE) for 150 metres, following cairns onto the ridge (55M) from where we have clear views of the southern plain and **Alcúdia Bay**. Bearing left (another path on the left lower down can also be taken), we follow the ridge

(NE) soon coming into view of the summit and its trig point (NOT the small summit with a pole at the top of the curving valley).

Following the cairns across largely pathless limestone brings us back into sight of **Puigs Roig** and **Caragoler de Femenia** on our left (Wp.5 65M), after which a gentle climb on rough ground leads to the summit (Wp.6 75M) from where we have superb views down the **Pollença** valley. Behind **Pollença**, the first small hump is **Serra de la Coma**, the sharp peak is the **Cuculla de Fartatrix**, and the large block-like mountain below us is **Puig de Ca**, our next objective.

First though, we descend to

the **Casa Neu** or **Snow House**, clearly visible to the south-east, where there is a grassy windbreak tucked behind the snow-gatherers' cabin (Wp.7 80M). Beyond the cabin there's a splendid snow-pit, 20 metres to the right of which, a red arrow and cairns indicate our way down. Following the cairns, red dots and occasional stretches of path, we descend in a south-easterly direction before bearing left (NNE).

fungi below Serra d'en Massot

A steady descent leads to a large grey metal post (Wp.8 100M) where we leave the clear trail and turn sharp right, following the cairns to scramble down onto the western limit of the **Coll del Puig de Ca**. Crossing the *coll* (E) we join a faint track (Wp.9 115M) near the wall climbing from the far side of the *coll* to the *puig*.

Turning right, we follow the track over a grassy rise, where it starts descending, skirting the fenced depression of **Clot Fondo** and running into a better-stabilised, partially concreted track down to the **Es Rafal** junction (Wp.10 135M), visible for most of our descent from Wp.9. Bearing right, we follow the main track across the broad plain of **Camp Redo**. When the track ends in a turning circle (Wp.11 145M), we head for a large ladder-stile and a gap in the fence. Beyond the fence, a narrow path winds through large clumps of *carritx* (SW) passing occasional cairns and crossing the odd outcrop of rock, making its way to the head of a narrow valley (Wp.12 165M), at the top of which there are numerous pleasant picnic spots.

We meander through the valley, following cairns when the path disappears in the undergrowth, before descending to pass under two large oaks, 100 metres after which we come to a new fence and ladder-stile (Wp.13 185M).

Crossing the stile, we follow a broad stony trail leading to a dirt track behind the **Aucanella** (AKA **Alcanella**) farmhouse (invisible on this route). Bearing right, we follow the track, crossing another new fence and stile, 100 metres after which we cross the signposted path taken in Walk 32.

We can either follow the signposts or continue along the track as it winds round to a flat area with a ruined shelter sandwiched between the rocks on our left. Leaving the flat area, the track climbs slightly through an S-bend, just after which there's a large oak (Wp.14 200M).

At this point we intersect with Walks 32 & 24. We can return to **Binifaldó** via the torrent featured in Walk 32, the off path-route of Walk 24, or (recommended) the end of Walk 24. For a description of this route, see Walk 24 Wps.7-11. Walk 24 Wps.8-11 have been appended to the waypoint file of the present itinerary.)

Puig Major being off limits due to the military installations on the top, **Puig de Massanella** is Mallorca's highest accessible summit, and in this itinerary we follow the classic route to the top via the **Comafreda** estate.

It's a paying route (6 euros for foreigners), but for peak baggers and vista seekers, this is a small price to pay on an island where access is a perennial problem. Despite being the most domestic route to the top, this is rough walking only recommended for experienced walkers.

Massanella seen from Canaleta (Walk 18)

5 | 4-5 H | 11 km | 800m / 800m | out & back | 0

Access: by car or bus. The walk starts just beyond the bridge on the MA2130 south of the petrol station on **Coll de sa Bataia** above **Lluc**. If arriving by car, park opposite the petrol station. If arriving by bus (L330 between **Palma** and **Lluc**, L354 between **Sóller** and **Pollença**), ask to be dropped off at the **Coll de sa Bataia** *gasolinera*.

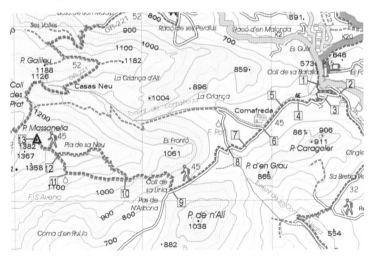

Immediately after the bridge south of the petrol station, we take the broad, gated track to the west of the road (Wp.1 0M). Doubling back to the right at junctions 200 and 400 metres from the road (Wps.2 & 3), we climb to the **Comafreda** farm toll booth (Wp.4 24M). Continuing along the main track, we pass a branch on the left (Wp.5), then turn left in front of the farmhouse on a broad, shady trail dotted with red waymarks (Wp.6 35M).

After going through a gap in a wall (Wp.7 43M), the trail dwindles to a rocky path that climbs to join a dirt track (Wp.8 51M), where we turn left. We now simply follow this track up to the clearing on the **Coll de sa Linea** where there are two large stone marker posts (Wp.9 62M). Turning right, we take a clear path between the marker posts that climbs through the woods to a triangular concrete marker post (Wp.10 86M) indicating 'Font y Puig' on the left and 'Puig y Font' on the right (the font in question being the **Font de s'Avenc** spring).

The second option is the easier way to the top, but if you want to do both routes, I suggest passing by the **S'Avenc** spring first as a steep climb is less risky than a steep descent. Beware, though: the spring route traverses rough, pathless terrain, and there's a maze of divergent, cairn marked ways, most of which go nowhere. Always follow the lower route marked with cairns AND red waymarks. If you find the cairns are getting increasingly infrequent and the waymarks have disappeared, you're on a false trail. Go back till you find regular cairns and waymarks. Particular care must be taken in the first 200 metres after the marker stone. Leastways, that's where I got lost!

Staying more or less on the level and only climbing slightly, never steeply, we follow the cairns and waymarks (W) until we pass a large bushy oak, beyond which the real climb begins, initially on rubble, but soon passing a sloping rock shelf with five marker steps cemented onto it. A steady climb across the rocks, passing waymarks, cairns and the occasional cemented marker step brings us abreast of the **Font de s'Avenc** (Wp.11 107M), where steps descend to the spring and a damp shelter with rough stone benches and a table.

Just after the spring, cairns mark the way up the jagged limestone crowning the mountain. A steep climb gradually brings us into view of the trig point on the peak. After passing another triangular marker stone (Wp.12 122M), the gradient eases briefly and, 100 metres later, we join the easier path from the **Pla de sa Neu** or Snow Plain, where we bear left for the final slog up to the summit (Wp.13 142M).

After taking in the views and staying well back from the alarming drops on the northern side of the summit, we retrace our way back to the easier route across the **Pla de sa Neu** (E), at the end of which the trail bears right (SSE) to go through a natural gateway onto a good path zigzagging down to Wp.10 (162M), from where we return to the start via the same route.

Massanella, seen from the south

If you only have time for one itinerary on the **Alcúdia Peninsula**, this is probably the one to opt for (though Walks 12 & 35 are complementary), combining wild terrain, a strenuous climb, grand views, and a good feed at the end. The griddled cuttlefish (*sepia a la plancha*) at the **S'Illot** restaurant is particularly recommended.

Extension	Short Version	Stroll
Penya Roja and **Puig Romani** (see text). Add 130 metres climbing.	**Penya Roja** and **Puig Romani** from the **Ermita de la Victoria** car park.	If you want a peaceful picnic spot not far from the road, descend directly into the streambed at Wp.1 and follow its course until the silence and isolation seem total.

Access: by car, bike or (adding 3km) bus (L356b from **Alcúdia**). From **Alcúdia**, take the **Mal Pas** road and follow the ermita sign to the left of the **Bodega del Sol Bar**. The walk begins at the **S'Illot** bar/restaurante, 1.5km after the **Mal Pas** bus stop.

50 metres after the restaurant, directly in front of the islet from which it takes its name, we walk up the youth hostel driveway and, 25 metres from the road, take the path off to the left (Wp.1 0M), immediately bearing right. The path climbs steadily, shadowing the driveway, then crosses a runoff channel (Wp.2 6M) where it levels out and broadens to a track.

Bearing right, we stay on the main track (SW) until it joins another, wayposted track beside a roughly concreted culvert (Wp.3 14M), where we turn right, then left 50 metres later (Wp.4) for 'Coll de na Benet, Alcúdia'. Ignoring minor branches off to the right, we follow the wayposted track towards a large hilltop villa with a lookout tower, soon bringing the folds of the **Ses Fontanelles** valley into view. We join Walk 12 (Wp.2) at a waymarked junction with a path doubling back to the right, where we carry straight on (Wp.5 27M).

The track crosses the **Ses Fontanelles** torrent beside a mini-dam and we turn right (Wp.6 29M) on a signposted path for 'Coll de na Benet'. The path climbs alongside the torrent in easy stages, crossing its course four times, before a slightly steeper ascent brings us onto the **Coll de na Benet** (Wp.7 44M), where we turn left for the ascent shared with Walk 35.

approaching the Talaia

At first we appear to be heading into pathless scrub, but after a few metres a faint trail (largely pioneered by goats but marked by man with cairns and the occasional red dot) becomes clear, winding through the *carritx* toward the **Talaia**, which is clearly visible for most of the ascent. A steady climb brings us to a small coll, after which the ascent becomes visibly steeper and the path dwindles to a cairn-marked way over bare rock (Wp.8 56M).

view from the top

After an initial climb along the central spine, we follow a patch of path on the southern flank, at the end of which (Wp.9 60M), we clamber across the rocks back onto the central spine.

Zigzagging back and forth to break the gradient, but maintaining a northeasterly direction, we climb steeply to reach the foot of the summit crag (Wp.10 80M), where we can either scramble directly over the rocks onto the summit, or skirt left to join the main summit path just above a signpost indicating the descents to the *ermita* (on the left) and 'Coll Baix' (on the right) (Wp.11 87M).

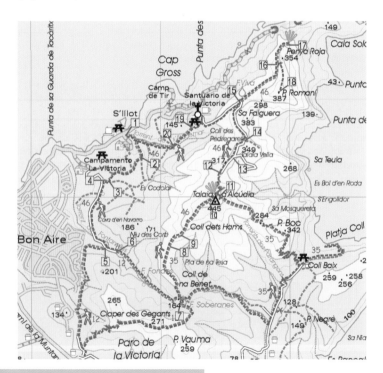

Bearing left, we follow the main path as it drops through some dramatic zigzags (slippery when wet) to a stand of pine, below which the path runs into the broad track (Wp.12 95M) down to the *ermita*. Following the main track, we ignore forks descending and climbing to the right (Wp.13 & 14) and descend to a U-bend so tight it's almost a loop, above which steps and wooden railings mark the start of our extension (Wp.15 106M).

EXTENSION: The branch path climbs steadily round the northern side of the peninsula, levelling out briefly before descending then climbing alongside the crags below **Puig Romani** to a junction (Wp.16 15M from Wp.15). For **Penya Roja**, we take the path to the left, which runs alongside the cliffs to fortifications overlooking **Cap Pinar**.

Squeezing through a tunnel-like entrance, we negotiate a slightly vertiginous section (very vertiginous on the way back) with the help of a chain set in the rocks, and descend to a natural *mirador* amid the defensive works (Wp.17 5M from Wp.16). For **Puig Romani**, we bear right at Wp.16 and climb steeply to the **Penya des Migdia** coll, where we turn sharp right and scramble onto the summit (Wp.18 15M from Wp.16) to enjoy glorious views, including the somewhat improbable sight of a canon perched on **Penya Roja**. In both cases, we return to Wp.15 via the same route. Timings for the extension are not counted at subsequent waypoints.

To return to the start, we simply follow the main track down to the *ermita*.

Immediately before the carpark (Wp.19 116M), we turn left on the badly eroded 'Campament, Benet, Alcúdia' path.

The path curls round below the carpark then descends into a densely wooded valley where it crosses the **Aladernar** torrent, immediately after which we leave the signposted path, turning right to descend into the torrent itself (Wp.20 123M), which we follow back to our starting point and a good feed.

descending the torrent at the end

The **Camí des Correu** or 'Mail Path' between **Banyalbufar** and **Esporles** is a fabulous trail, traversing one of the loveliest oak woods on the island. It's a popular route, but every time I do it, I'm taken aback by just how lovely it is and can understand all too well why so many people, plenty of them clearly not habitual walkers, regard this excursion as an essential Sunday afternoon outing.

Combined with Walk 28, it makes for one of the most memorable day walks on the island. However, the climb out of **Banyalbufar** is steep and can seem interminable on a hot afternoon, so you may wish to use the bus and enjoy two half-day excursions. With one notable exception, all major junctions are well signposted and, once you're on-trail, description is virtually superfluous, which is all to the good, since it would be a shame to be reading about this lovely trail rather than simply enjoying it.

3 | 2H | 7.7 km | 360m / 260m | one way | 5*

* in the villages

Access: by bus; the two towns are linked by the hourly L200 service from **Palma**.

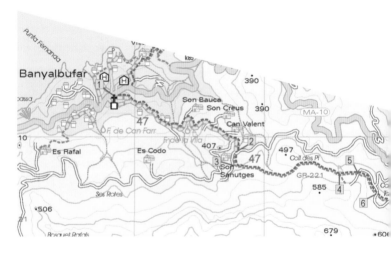

We set off from **Plaza de la Vila**, the elevated square in front of the *ayuntamiento* directly above **Banyalbufar**'s central bus-stops, on the narrow street climbing to the left of the town hall, **Carrer Jeroni Alberti** (Wp.1 0M). Jeroni Alberti becomes **Carrer de Font de la Vila** and we pass a GR sign on the wall announcing 'Esporles Camí des Correu 2h30', after which we leave the housing behind and the street becomes an attractive lane climbing steeply into the terraced countryside surrounding the village.

We follow this lane <u>all</u> the way to the <u>very</u> end (you'll soon understand the emphasis), climbing steadily to steeply, ignoring all branch tracks and paths. After what seems like forever (in fact, only one-and-a-half kilometres), we pass the entrance to **Can Valent,** and the tarmac gives way to concrete for the last couple of hundred metres, at the end of which we come to a crossroads with a dirt track on the edge of the **Son Sanutges** estate (Wp.2 29M).

Carrying straight on, we cross the dirt track and follow a signposted trail, concreted for the first few metres and broad enough to look like a track, but soon dwindling to the intermittently cobbled trail of the **Camí des Correu**. The trail runs alongside the **Son Sanutges** fence, swinging left at a junction with the dirt track on the far side of the fence (Wp.3 33M), after which we enter the Holm Oak wood. The *camí* continues to climb steadily for the first couple of hundred metres, then levels off as we cross two broken walls.

approaching Coll des Pi

At this point, you will begin to appreciate why it was worth slogging up that lane, and why quite so many people regard this path as a good reason to skip church, visiting the relatives, having a nap in front of the TV, stuffing themselves silly with *paella*, or whatever other Sunday inactivity you care to name.

After a stroll so sweet it could provoke diabetes, we come to a long section of paved trail that climbs gently into woodland where the pine predominate, though there are also plenty of strawberry

Son Bunyola

trees, and we cross, probably without noticing, the appropriately named **Coll des Pi**.

After the imperceptible *coll*, the *camí* levels off again and views open out over the coast down toward **Port des Canonge** and the big block-like manor house of **Son Bunyola**, formerly Richard Branson's little place in the country and more recently the object of a money laundering scandal involving a man named Hoare - honestly, I read it in the papers.

Sa Foradada

The woodland soon closes in again, cutting off the views except for brief glimpses through the trees. Passing an ancient, obscure trail doubling back to the right (Wp.4 54M) and, 50 metres later, a particularly fine limekiln, we continue with our cultivation of an ever more acute case of diabetes.

cliffs north of Puig Veia

Carrying straight on at a crossroads with a dirt track (Wp.5 57M) and a broad trail (Wp.6 62M), we cross another imperceptible *coll* (**Coll de sa Talaieta**) at a sign indicating 'Esporles 40m'.

We now descend through a series of zigzags to a long straight stretch leading to a patch of paving, at the end of which we carry straight on (Wp.7 71M) alongside a wall for a final descent through the woods. After passing another limekiln and two very faint paths forking off to the right within 50 metres of one another (so faint you may not even notice them) (Wp.8 77M), we go through a gate, beyond which the woodland gives way to abandoned terraces.

A couple of hundred metres after a second gate, the trail emerges on the MA-1120 (Wp.9 89M). Crossing the road, we follow a newly made path shadowing the road past the turning to 'Puigpunyent' and 'La Granja', a large country house that is now a popular tourist attraction. 50 metres after a bend in the old road, we recross the MA-1120 (Wp.10 100M) to join a dirt track climbing to a Y-junction in front of a gate into a field (Wp.11 105M).

Forking right, we follow a bridleway that brings us into **Esporles** at the bend of a lane behind the church (Wp.12 111M). Carrying straight on, we descend to the church, where we bear left, passing in front of the **Hotel l'Estada** to join the main road in front of the **Esporles** *ayuntamiento* (Wp.13 114M).

Stage 4a of the GR221 between **Esporles** and **Valldemossa** is a bucolic excursion traversing a charming pastoral landscape and a wild, little visited woodland. Unfortunately, a dispute about hunting rights has lead local landowners to fence off the path between the **Coll de sa Basseta** and the **Coll de San Jordi**. Fortunately, this does not effect the eastern end of the stage, so contrary to the other GR itineraries in the book, in this outing we walk east to west, climbing onto the **Sa Comuna** ridge, from where we enjoy superb views of the **Teix** massif, the **Molas de Son Ferrandell** and **Son Pacs**, and the wide expanse of the azure blue sea, not only to the north, but to the south, too.

* in Valldemossa **Stroll**:- Molide sa Beata

Access: on foot from **Valldemossa**. Our itinerary starts at the northern end of **Valldemossa**, just opposite the bus stop and large coachpark where the MA1110 becomes the MA1130 (Wp.1 0M).

Es Molinet

From Wp.1, we take **Carrer de Uruguay** toward the **Reial Cartuja**, turning right 30 metres later between houses Nºs1 & 2 to head toward the distinctive turret of the **Es Molinet** windmill, now a private house

Immediately behind the mill, tucked into a small parking bay (Wp.2 3M), we take a narrow path climbing onto the northern flank of the **Moli de sa Beata**, a wooded hill topped with the eponymous mill.

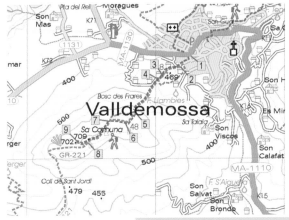

the trail after Wp.4

A gentle climb brings us to a junction with a stepped path climbing left to the top of the *moli*, but we fork right twice (Wp.3 8M) to reach the corner of a house and a gateway into the **Font de na Llambies** (Wp.4 9M). Going through the gateway, we climb behind the house along a partially cobbled trail.

After climbing steadily then steeply alongside a boundary wall, we go through a waymarked gap in another wall to reach a glade where there is a ruin, a covered cistern and a GR waypost (Wp.5 22M).

The path splits into two forks here. For the present, we leave

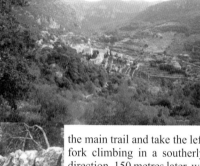

Valldemosa seen after Wp.4

the main trail and take the left fork climbing in a southerly direction. 150 metres later, we ignore a faint path off to the left and cross the principal boundary wall via stone steps set in the wall (Wp.6 26M). Strolling through the woods, we soon rejoin the main trail beside another cistern (Wp.7 29M), where we turn left to climb onto the main ridge.

Waypoint 6

Once on the top, where you turn back is a matter of taste as the various vantage points (south to **Palma**, the plain, and the port, north to the great expanse of blue beyond **Port de Valldemossa**, east to **Teix**, and west to the *molas*) are all equally attractive. To reach the highest point along the ridge, we stick with the main path as it winds through the woods until it crosses a broken wall beside a roofed corral. 50 metres after passing a second roofed corral, the path starts to descend more steeply, at which point we fork right (Wp.8 39M) and climb across bare rock to reach an unmarked rocky outcrop (Wp.9) take care though as there's a nasty little drop on the far side.

We return the same way with the options of staying on the main trail at Wp.7 to reach Wp.5 via a gate in the wall, and turning right at Wp.4 to circle the **Moli de sa Beata**.

This is one of the most remarkable stretches of the **Dry Stone Way**, incorporating both the **Archduke's Path** (see Walk 40) and the extraordinary descent to **Deià** via the **Cingles de Rullan**. There is a slight risk of vertigo, but not acute (I suffer from vertigo and classify this walk as a toe tingler), and for anyone who loves spectacular paths and stunning views, this is a walk in the MUST DO category. Worth the plane fare all on its own. If you're short of time, this itinerary could be combined with Walk 50 to make a single long itinerary.

4 | 3H | 7.9 km | 520m one way | 800m | ⚠ | 5*

* in Valledemossa & Deià

Access: by bus. **Valldemossa** and **Deià** are linked by the L210 service from **Palma**, which runs every two hours and also serves Sóller.

From the bus-stop at the northern end of **Valldemossa**, the point at which the MA-1110 becomes the MA-1130 (Wp.1 0M), we cross the **Plaça Camp de Vànol** and carry straight on along the road behind the taxi stand. 75 metres later, we take the second turning on the right (Wp.2) to pass the sports field, beyond which we continue on **Carrer de Joan Fuster**. We then fork left into **Carrer de Oliveres** (Wp.3), at the end of which a broad walking trail begins beside the gates of the **Son Gual Petit** *finca* (Wp.4 8M). The trail shadows the **Son Gual** driveway, then swings left, climbing to cross a stile (Wp.5 13M), where we ignore branches off to left and right. Thereafter, we climb steadily along a beautifully graded trail winding through sun-dappled woodland.

Pla des Pouet

There are a number of shortcuts across bends toward the top, but they serve no great purpose, apart perhaps from encouraging erosion, so we stick with the main route until it goes through a gateway into a flat, wooded area, the **Pla des Pouet**, at the heart of which, 200 metres from the gateway, there's a junction of

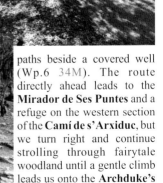

paths beside a covered well (Wp.6 34M). The route directly ahead leads to the **Mirador de Ses Puntes** and a refuge on the western section of the **Camí de s'Arxiduc**, but we turn right and continue strolling through fairytale woodland until a gentle climb leads us onto the **Archduke's Path** at the **Coll de Son**

waypoint 7

Gallard, where there is a long V-shaped bench (Wp.7 49M). Turning right, we continue our gentle climb, with intermittent views back to the west opening out.

After crossing a broken down wall, we climb more steeply to a junction with a broader stretch of the bridleway (Wp.8 56M), where we turn left.

Brace yourselves; 200 metres later, we emerge on a superb natural *mirador* overlooking, off to the left, the refuge on **Puig Veia**, and off to the right, the **Cingles de Son Rullan** - that's right, the ones we descend!

Don't worry, though, the descent is not via the near cliffs, which are sheer, but the

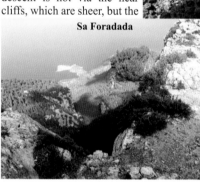

Puig Veia

Sa Foradada

more distant drop, clad in woodland.

Continuing on the most spectacular part of the bridleway (toes-tingling, no doubt), **Teix** comes into view, and a fine perspective opens out onto the pierced rock of **Sa Foradada** on the coast.

After contouring along the edge of the cliffs, we climb across what appears to be a discrete summit, but is in fact the western edge of a plateau preceding the diminutive but distinctively conical peak of **Puig des Caragolí**.

At this stage, **Puig Major**, Mallorca's highest mountain, comes into view, and we can make out new white housing climbing the eastern flank of **Port de Sóller**.

waypoint 9

Ten metres after passing a large pile of stones and a couple of hundred metres short of **Puig des Caragoli**,

the Archduke's Path

we turn left between two large cairns (Wp.9 78M), leaving the **Archduke's Path** and embarking on the second bit of the day's adventure.

From this perspective, it looks to all intents and purposes as if we're just going to walk off the edge of a cliff, which we are in a way, though not in a manner necessarily detrimental to health. Following a clear, stony path waymarked with cairns and another large pile of stones, we descend gently (NE), passing to the right of the main clump of Holm Oak, where a flurry of cairns marks the head of the *cingles* path (Wp.10 85M).

the *cingles* pathfrom Wp.10

(**NB** A couple of people have gone astray between Wps.9 & 10, veering off to the right on an alternative cairn marked route. It's worth emphasizing that we head NNE to the cliff path rather than trekking down the scar edge).

A word to the wise: GPS reception can be poor below these cliffs, but for the next 40 minutes, GPS is strictly for the birds given that anybody trying to maintain a straight line will have to fly.

After a first long sloping shelf descending steeply amid Holm Oak in an easterly direction, the path veers round to the west on a slightly exposed section then zigzags down to what appears to be another sheer drop, but is in fact another long, easterly traverse, once again shielded by Holm Oak.

Immediately after skirting a large rock sticking up in the middle of the path (Wp.11 103M), we pass a gatepost built into the cliff, presumably the remains of a counting gate when descending shepherds checked they still had their entire flock, and fine views open out over the **Son Rullan** farmhouse. 150 metres later, we must take care to double back to the right along the cairn-marked path when a minor branch carries straight on (Wp.12). The woods become denser and deeper as we continue our descent, but we still have to pause to appreciate their beauty, as the rough path means we must watch every step of the way.

After countless zigzags (possibly somebody's counted them, but it's not the sort of pastime that gets my pulse racing), we pass a *sitja* and the remains of a charcoal burner's cabin (Wp.13 115M).

Still winding back and forth like an epileptic snake, the path crosses a second *sitja*, then joins a broader path at a 3rd *sitja* beside a bread oven (Wp.14 120M).

Bearing right and crossing the *sitja*, we pass a trough carved into a massive boulder and an interesting combination of a *sitja* and limekiln side by side.

bread oven at waypoint 14

the *sitja* & limekiln

Sticking with the cairn-marked route, we ignore two branches off to the right (Wps.15 & 16 127M), after which the woodland thins and

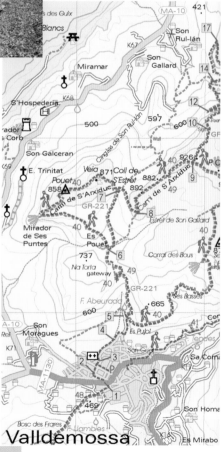

pine predominate, and we emerge on a long terrace within sight of **Deià**.

Reaching a gateway in a wall with two very ramshackle rusting gates hanging from their hinges like a couple of sagging drunks (Wp.17 133M), we double back to the right on a narrow initially cobbled path. Look out for the cairns here as this path is increasingly invaded by *carritx* and could disappear altogether if it's not cleared.

We zigzag down across terraces, forking left on another cobbled stretch 75 metres before a cabin (visible from the first terrace after Wp.16) (Wp.18 137M), passing a small spring and trough, immediately after which we again fork left (Wp.19).

We now descend on an intermittently cobbled path along the delightful little valley (once cultivated but now abandoned to the

Castell des Moro

carritx) that divides the dilapidated stronghold of **Castell des Moro** from the **Can Borràs** farmhouse.

The path eventually joins a dirt track in front of **Can Borràs** (Wp.20 159M).

Bearing right, we follow this track and the lane it leads into all the way down to the **Hotel Es Molí** car-park, ignoring all branches en route. Directly in front of the hotel, we take the **Camí de Ca'n Quet** stairway (Wp.21 168M).

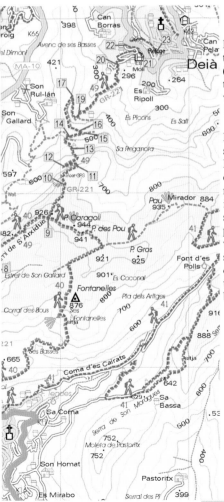

Emerging on the road (Wp.22), we turn left then right 50 metres later (Wp.23 172M) on a lane that leads to the **Can Boi** refuge at the head of valley below the village (Wp.24 177M).

For Walk 50 and to reach the bus stop, which is on the far side of **Deià**, take the one way street climbing to the west from the refuge. Turn left after 150 metres into **Calle Es Teix** then carry straight on after 30 metres on the pedestrianized **Calle na Topa**, which leads into the village's main street. After passing the post office, descend to the left of **Can Blau** to the MA10. Walk 50 is on the left, the bus stop on the right.

Possibly one of the most popular paths in Mallorca, the linear route between **Deià** and **Sóller** via **Can Prohom** was the obvious choice for this stretch of the **GR221**. It features some lovely trails, enviable cabins and farmhouses, and superb views, and is marred only by an inexplicable stretch of road walking between Wps.6&7.

Access: by bus. **Sóller** and **Deià** are linked by the L210 service from **Palma**, which runs every two hours. The walk starts to the north of the **Deià** bus stop just beyond the main car park on the MA10.

From the eastern end of **Deià**, just beyond the main car park, we take the **Camí de sa Vinyeta** (Wp.1 0M), a tarmac lane descending on the left toward the primary school. At the end of the lane, we go through a gate (Wp.2 3M) and follow a broad trail zigzagging down terraces of olive trees. The *camí* crosses the **Cala Deià** road three times before joining it 30 metres short of the **Camí de Ribassos** footbridge, immediately in front of which, we climb to the right (Wp.3 14M).

the footbridge at Wp.3

Following a broad trail, we climb steadily out of the **Torrent Major** gorge.150 metres after the path levels out, we veer right (Wp.4 21M) and climb gently to join a dirt track, on which we maintain direction (NE), forking right after 100 metres to pass behind a small byre (Wp.5), immediately after which we

bear left to cross a cattle grid at the lower end of a surfaced lane. Toward the top of the lane, ignore the little stub of wayposted trail climbing to the right (it only adds 25 metres to the road walking and lands you in the middle of a particularly hair raising bend) and stay on the lane to join the MA10 (Wp.6 28M), which we follow to the left.

Cala de Deià gorge

After 400 metres, we turn right on a stepped trail signposted **Cami de Castello** (Wp.7 32M). The trail runs into a lane 50 metres later. Following the wayposted route, we climb steeply until the lane veers right and passes behind the garden and swimming pool of **Can Rosel**, where we turn left (Wp.8 36M) on a broad dirt trail. After a short but steady climb, the path levels out briefly, then a succession of long, shallow steps takes us onto higher ground where the path is flanked by a series of cabins and small houses, the most substantial of which, **Son Coll** (Wp.9 53M), abuts directly onto the path. A long, recently paved stretch (slippery when wet) brings us down to a junction with a dirt track and, to the left, a signposted path for 'Font de ses Mentides' (Wp.10 55M). Bearing right, we recover the old cobbled trail as it climbs to cross a tiny lane (Wp.11 58M).

the threshing circle above Wp,12

After a pleasant stroll along a shady woodland terrace, the trail dips down to cross a watercourse, then climbs briefly before a final level stretch brings us back into a more classic cultivated landscape of olive, oleaster and carob tree terraces. Crossing a track behind a large threshing circle and shallow aljub, we drop down to join a

dirt track (Wp.12 78M) that we follow down to the right to a large eighteenth century farmhouse, commonly known as **Can Prohom**. In fact, **Can Prohom** is only the eastern wing of the house. The western wing, **Son Mico**, is a guest house serving coffee and orange juice, and some very tempting looking tarts.

Son Micó

Crossing the courtyard in front of the main building, we follow a cobbled trail down to a derelict chapel (Wp.13 81M), where we turn left to descend to the MA10 in front of the **Son Bleda Hotel**/bar/restaurant (Wp.14 85M). NB If you're staying in **Sóller** and want to descend directly, the town can be reached by pleasant sign and wayposted routes carrying straight on at Wp.13. See Walk 17 Wp.12.

views west from Ben d'Avalls lane

Turning left in front of **Son Bleda** and taking great care (there's a nasty little bend ahead), we follow the MA10 for 125 metres then turn right on the **Bens d'Avall** lane (Wp.15). When the main lane climbs slightly then descends sharp left some 600 metres later, we turn right on a track (surfaced for the first 50

metres) (Wp.16 97M). Bearing right (Wp.17) then left (Wp.18 101M) at the next two junctions, we wind through olive groves, individual trees looking so gnarled and ancient you can well believe some have been carbon dated BC.

Reaching a 'Camina per Mallorca' mapboard, we maintain direction (E) for 'Port de Sóller' (Wp.19 110M), then carry straight again on at a crossroads 75 metres later (Wp.20) before forking right 25 metres after that (Wp.21) on a wayposted path that curves round the **Muleta de Cats Avinyons** farmhouse. Behind the farmhouse, we turn sharp left on a narrow path (Wp.22 115M) into another ancient olive grove.

Following a broad trail peppered with cairns, we join a cobbled way that dips down into a swale then crosses a rise from where views open out over **Port de Sóller**. Passing the **Muleta de ca s'Hereu** farmhouse (where they sell orange juice and *pa amb oli*) (Wp.23 124M), we trace a horseshoe curve round the next gully then descend to go through one more olive grove (Wps.24 & 25 130M & 133M), after which a good cobbled trail brings us down to a signposted junction behind the derelict **Hotel Rocamar** (Wp.26 141M).

For **Port de Sóller**, turn sharp left here and cross the hotel via a dirt track leading to the PMV113, 500 metres from the seafront.
For **Sóller**, we carry straight on.
Forking right at the next junction (Wp.27 146M), we go through a gate to follow a terrace path behind a private house.
After climbing briefly below cliffs so heavily mottled they look like they've been

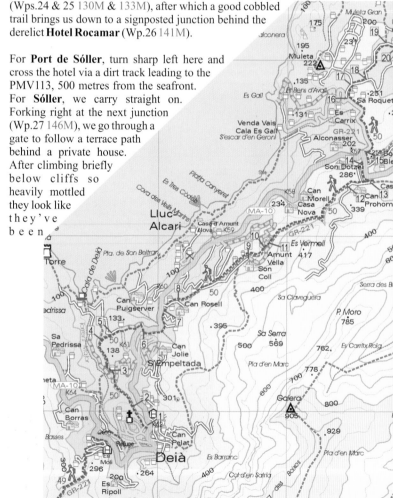

approaching the Son Sales valley

camouflaged, we descend into the **Son Sales** valley, bearing right when our path feeds into a dirt track (Wp.28 158M) leading to a narrow tarmac lane (Wp.29 161M), the **Camí de Son Sales**. Turning left, we pass the **Hotel Can n'Ai** and follow the lane till it ends a kilometre later (Wp.30 163M). The L210 stops down to the left here.

Alternatively, to return to the centre of **Sóller** via the GR, we turn right at the end of the **Camí de Son Sales**, then left 75 metres later (Wp.31), and follow a minor road that joins the **Sóller** bypass at a roundabout (Wp.32). We cross the bypass, turn right, then fork left 100 metres later onto the **Camí des Camp Llarg** (unnamed at this end).

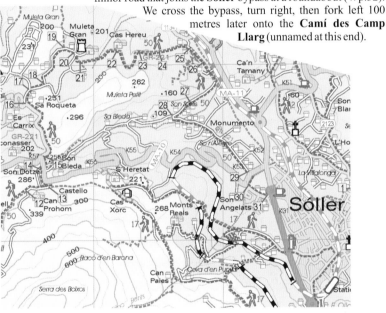

When the **Camí des Camp Llarg** crosses **Carrer Cetre** (the broad road with the **Agrotec** outlet), we turn left, then right into the **Camí de sa Mar**. At the top of the **Camí de sa Mar**, we turn left into **Carrer de la Rectoria** to reach **Sóller**'s central **Placa de sa Constituçio**.

Placa de sa Constitució

For those who don't have time to do the full **Dry Stone Way**, but fancy an overnight walk that takes in some of the very finest paths on the island and some of the most spectacular terrain, this variant on Stages 6 & 7 of the **GR221** is the perfect itinerary, climbing the classic **Barranc de Biniaraix** donkey trail to the **Cúber** reservoir, then branching off the GR to reach the **Refuge de Tossals Verds** via the inappropriately named **Pas Llis** (there's nothing 'smooth' about it) before circling round the **Tossals Verds** massif and redescending the **Barranc de Biniaraix**. Exceptional walking, but only for experienced walkers as we explore some wild and little visited terrain. There is a slight risk of vertigo. If you're staying overnight at the refuge, it is essential to book in advance, either on line (see the hiking page of the Consell de Mallorca site **http://www.conselldemallorca.net/**) or by phone 971 173 700 or 971 173 701.

STOP PRESS: At the time of going to press, news arrived that the route between **Cúber** and **Tossals Verds via Pas Llis** has been signposted.

DAY 1 SÓLLER to TOSSALS VERDS via Pas Llis

5 | 5¼ H | 15.3 km | 1030m / 550m | one way | 4*

* at the Refuge de Tossals Verds

Access: on foot from **Sóller**. To reach the start from **Sóller**'s central **Plaça de sa Constitucio**, take **Carrer de sa Luna** beside the BBVA bank on the far side of the plaza, then turn left into **Carrer de la Victoria 11 Maig**. Carrying straight on at the crossroads, fork right at the bridge, signposted 'Piscina Municipal'. The football field is on the right, 300 metres later, at the junction with the **Fornalutx** road.

From **Sóller** football ground (Wp.1 0M), we follow the 'Fornalutx' road for 200 metres then turn left at a '*Camina per Mallorca*' mapboard onto a minor lane (Wp.2). We stick with the lane when it swings right 100 metres later at a junction with a surfaced track (Wp.3) and ignore a track forking off to the left after another 200 metres, when the lane becomes the **Camí de s'Ermita** (Wp.4 7M). At the end of the lane (Wp.5 15M), we turn left then right 30 metres later (Wp.6) on a narrow cobbled path climbing to the lovely little hamlet of **Binibassi**. In the heart of the hamlet, the path becomes a lane again (Wp.7 20M) that we follow down to rejoin the **Fornalutx** road,

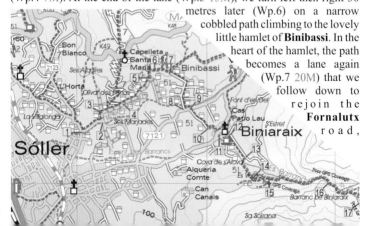

where we turn left (Wp.8 29M) then right at the bus-stop 50 metres later (Wp.9) into the **Camí Horta de Biniaraix**, another narrow lane that leads to a cobbled trail (Wp.10 34M) climbing into the village of **Biniaraix**.

Turning left on the village's minuscule main road (Wp.11 37M), we follow **Carrer de Sant Josep** round to the old *lavadero* and the start of the **Barranc de Biniaraix** dirt track (Wp.12 39M). When the *barranc* track bears left after 200 metres to go through a gate, we fork right (Wp.13) on a partially paved trail leading to the first of four ford/footbridge combinations that take us back and forth across the course of the torrent in the lower, cultivated quarter of the gorge. There's no call to be reading a book here as we now begin the steady slog up the two thousand steps said to feature in this trail, so it's simply a question of following the paved trail and pausing from time to time to take in the views unfolding behind us. The following text is simply for the purposes of pacing progress and giving you an idea of what to expect.

Ignoring two paths off to the right (Wp.14 & Wp.15 52M), we climb steadily amid a riot of rock, carob, olive and oleaster, the gorge narrowing the higher we go and offering an increasing number of tempting little plunge pools. After climbing alongside an ancient aquifer, we go through the narrow **S'Estret** declivity and cross a stone bridge (Wp.16 73M), then re-cross the torrent 100 metres later via the third ford/footbridge combination. After passing two small houses, **Can Silles** and **Can Sivella** (Wp.17 83M), the trail veers away from the torrent and zigzags up amid pine and oleaster, passing two impressive overhangs of water-streaked rock as a superb panorama over the **Sóller** plain opens out behind us. Eventually, the trail levels off below a third overhang and we go through a gate (Wp.18 108M) into the **Ofre** estate - don't be alarmed by the *'Toros Bravos'* sign . . . you'd have to be a very *bravo toro* to tackle all the hikers who come through here and the only bovines I've ever seen on the **Ofre** estate were a couple of uncommonly placid cows.

Compared to the stiff climb up the cobbled trail, we now enjoy an easy stroll into the main bowl of the **Ofre** estate, passing a signposted turning on the right for the 'Mirador d'en Quesada / Es Cornadors' (Wp.19 117M). Thereafter, though, we go through a second gate and the climbing resumes on a rough trail heading toward the unmistakable conical peak of **Ofre**.

Joining a dirt track at a bend (Wp.20), we maintain a north-easterly direction, following the track for 250 metres until it goes through a sharp left-hand bend. Immediately after the bend, we turn right (Wp.21 126M) then left 10 metres later (Wp.22) on sign/wayposted paths that climb steadily through mixed Holm Oak and pine woods. We cross the track (Wp.23 131M) then rejoin it (Wp.24 137M) for 20 metres, before recovering the path at a wayposted left hand turn (Wp.25) for the final climb to **Coll de l'Ofre**, where there's a large cross stuck in a pile of stones (Wp.26 140M). Carrying straight on, we follow a clearly sign and wayposted path toward the **Cúber** reservoir. After a gentle descent, the path joins the main **Ofre** track directly in front of the **Binimorat** farmhouse (Wp.27 150M). Turning left, we follow this track to the reservoir, where we fork left to go through a gate (Wp.28 167M) and follow the raised embankment round the northern shore, circling the reservoir to reach the main access gates at its eastern end (Wp.29 193M).

From the gates of the **Cúber** reservoir (Wp.A29/B01 0M), we follow the obvious, signposted path to the right along the inside of the main fence for a little under 100-metres, crossing the end of a broken wall beside the second of two fire-hazard warning signs, at which point we turn right, ignoring a GR waypost indicating that we carry straight on (Wp.30). A rough path marked with cairns climbs steeply alongside the wall, then zigzags up via clear traverses to a gateway in another wall on the **Coll de sa Coma des Ases** (Wp.31 214M) where views open out over the **Almedrá** valley toward the sugar loaf mountains of **Alcaldena** and **Alaró**, and we can see the continuation of our path winding along the eastern flank of the valley. Descending steeply on a stony path, we cross the head of an affluent torrent, the **Coma des Ases** (Wp.32 223M), where there are the remains of a wrecked light aircraft, though these are rapidly being consumed by the elements - five years ago, it was patently a plane, now it's merely the frame of a metal box. The path levels out here, crossing a small pass 250 metres later (Wp.33 228M), after which it swings round to the right and we begin our descent toward the **Almedrá** torrent, on the far side of which we can see a covered aquifer, another classic link between **Cúber** and the **Tossals Verds** refuge (see Walk 31).

Zigzagging down on the nearside of a band of rock, we pass to the left of a tiny ruin (Wp.34 239M) then descend more steeply. The green fields visible at the end of the valley lie about a kilometre below the refuge. Within sight of one of the tunnels used on the aquifer route, the path levels out briefly to cross a long rockslide (Wp.35 246M), but the steep descent soon resumes, heading directly toward the tunnel and the torrent. Shortly after crossing a second rockslide (Wp.36 250M), a patch of path held in by a retaining wall squeezes behind a pine, bringing a second tunnel into view.

Passing below cliffs that bear a distant (possibly entirely fanciful) resemblance to the head of an elephant covered in carbuncles, we descend almost to the torrent, crossing a short, sloping outcrop of rock that's a hands and bottoms job, after which a brief climb brings us to the base of the **Pas Llis**, where plastic covered cables fixed securely into the rock help us climb across the impressive but not manifestly dangerous pass (Wp.37 259M).

The rough walking continues as we traverse exposed spines of eroded limestone and a slide of boulders, dipping up and down, and winding round the mountain below the glorious little crag of **Salt des Cans**, The Dogs' Leap! We then cross a second boulder

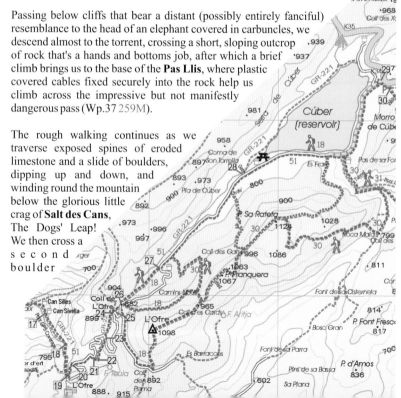

slide composed of rocks so large and menacing you'll probably be skipping across them with all the agility, rapidity, and levity of a May Fly (it's certainly not the sort of place to hang about loudly declaring your atheism), 50 metres after which, at a point where an arrow and the word **Cúber** have been daubed on the rock in red letters (Wp.38 270M), we pass on our left an off-path route descending from between the **Salt des Cans** and **Morro de sa Vaca** (something along the lines of 'The Cow's Snout'). A little over half a kilometre later, we cross a small rise and get our first glimpse of the roof of the refuge on the far side of the **Es Putxol** spine of rock (Wp.39 293M). Heading east, we follow a smooth path intermittently invaded by *carritx*, contouring round the lower reaches of the **Cases Velles** valley, and gradually descending onto terraces of olive and oleaster, where we go through a gateway (Wp.40 302M).

Crossing the valley on a good dirt path, we come to a junction marked with a GR-waypost (not the main route, but a variant via the **Cases Velles** valley) (Wp.41 309M), where we turn right to reach the refuge (Wp.42 313M).

the Refuge

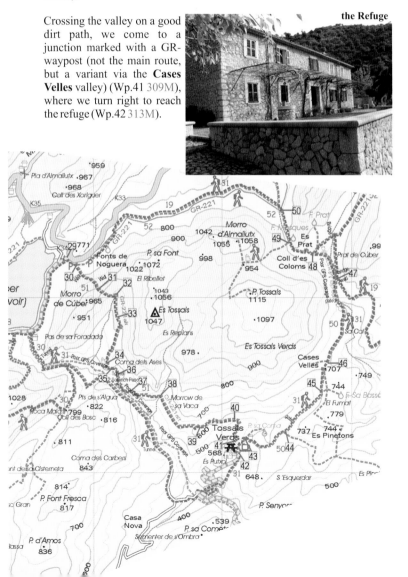

DAY 2 TOSSALS VERDS to SÓLLER via COLL D'ES COLLOMS

* at the Refuge

* It is possible to avoid re-walking the **Cúber-Binairaix** trail and thus reduce this part of the itinerary to a two hour, five kilometre hike with a 230 metre climb by catching the L354 bus at **Cúber** back to **Sóller**. It's a seasonal service and there is only one bus a day, so it's vital to check for up to date timetable information before setting off. Alternatively, you could make a longer day of it by exploring Walks 18, 19, or 30.

From the refuge (Wp.42 0M), we take the signposted path directly to the left of the main building for 'Font des Noguer 2h10, Font des Prat 1h10'. The broad, stony path climbs steadily, passing a signposted branch on the left for 'Pou de sa Coma' (Wp.43 6M), after which the gradient eases off as we approach the small conical summit of **Ses Cuculles**.

the signpost at waypoint 44

Carrying straight on at an intersection with a signposted way down to 'Mancor' (Wp.44 18M), we go through a gateway in a wall, from where we can see the head of the **Cases Velles** valley and the ruins themselves on the left. We carry straight on again at junctions with a path doubling back to the right (Wp.45 31M) and another on the left (Wp.46 36M).

After following a long, roughly cobbled trail, we eventually dip down to cross the **Torrent des Prat** via a ford (Wp.47 54M), 75 metres after which a bridge takes us back onto the torrent's right bank. 300 metres later, we reach a 'Camina per Mallorca' mapboard, signposted 'Font des Prat 10m Lluc 4h' (Wp.48 62M).

crossing the ford at Wp. 47

Bearing left, we continue on the main trail, passing a path on the left after another 300 metres (Wp.49 72M) as we cross the **Coll d'es Colloms**. We then descend to cross a bridge over a modern, concrete aqueduct between the **Cúber** reservoir and **Gorg Blau** (Wp.50 78M). Turning left, we follow the path alongside the aqueduct then cross the **Fonts de Noguera** car part to rejoin our outward route at Wp.30 (116M). We now follow the outward route back to **Sóller**.

This classic high mountain route combining parts of Stages 6 & 7 of the **GR221** was suggested to us as a discrete itinerary by reader Mike Williams. Apparently it's one of his wife's favourite walks. You can see why, too. There's a real high mountain feel to the traverse of the **Massanella** massif, the culminating point of the **Dry Stone Way**, the views are stunning, the recently restored **Camí de ses Voltes** trail is a gem, and we also pass some of the most impressive snowpits on the island.

* at Lluc

Access: by car and bus. Some logistical forethought required here as the walk relies on the L354 bus between **Sóller** and **Alcúdia**. It's a seasonal service (April to October) and runs once a day with a gap of about six hours for doing the walk. If arriving by bus, ask to be dropped off at **Cúber**. If arriving by car, park at **Cúber** (km34 of the MA10) or the **Font des Noguera** area recreativa 150 metres further east.

From the gates of the **Cúber** reservoir (Wp.1 0M), we follow the obvious, signposted path to the right along the inside of the main fence, crossing a stile into the **Font des Noguer** car-park a couple of hundred metres later (Wp.7). The spring and *área recreativa* are 100 metres directly ahead, otherwise we descend onto the road and bear right to reach a path signposted 'Font d'es Prat, Refugi des Tossals Verds' (Wp.3 5M). From here we embark on a pleasant stroll alongside a modern, open, concrete canal, enjoying fine views over the **Gorg Blau** reservoir. The canal feeds **Cúber** with the overflow from **Gorg Blau**, despite the fact that the latter is the lower of the two reservoirs.

After passing three concrete ramps bridging the aquifer, we cross it via the fourth ramp (Wp.4 37M), and go through a wooden gate to climb steadily through the woods on a partially stepped and intermittently cobbled donkey trail. The trail levels out on the **Coll d'es Coloms**, where we pass a path off to the right (Wp.5 44M). 300 metres later, we turn left for 'Font des Prat 10m, Lluc 4h' (Wp.6 52M).

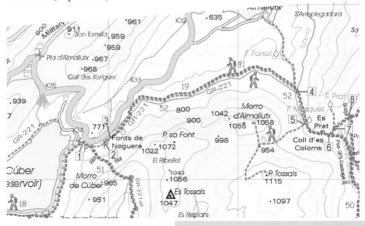

Font de ses Tosses d'en Gallina

After going through a gateway in a wall and passing a sheepfold, we ignore a fork off to the left (Wp.7) and carry straight on, passing single and twin *sitjes* to reach a signposted junction at a footbridge 50 metres south of the Font des Prat (Wp.8 57M).

Coll des Prat under snow!

Carrying straight on for 'Coll des ses Cases de sa Neu 1h30', another name for the **Coll des Prat**, the *cases de neu* being the snowpits previously used for stockpiling ice, we cross the footbridge and continue on a clear path climbing gently through the woods.

After a pleasant stroll through dense, mixed woodland, the landscape gradually changes, the pine and shrubs giving way to an underwood of boulders shadowed by mature Holm Oak, amid which the path levels out for 150 metres before passing a particularly large *sitja* and going through a gateway formed by the end of a wall and large blocks of rock (Wp.9 69M). We then resume climbing more steeply, the path begins to twist and turn to break the gradient, and the Holm Oak gradually give way to pine, between which we can glimpse the **Serra des Teixos** off to our left.

Forking right at Y-junctions with two shortcuts within 100 metres of each other (Wps.10 278M & 11) between which we pass the **Font de ses Tosses d'en Gallina** spring, we emerge from the woods and the **Coll des Prat** comes into view

the second snow-pit

directly ahead of us, framed by the rocky pinnacles of the **Serra des Teixos** and the massive bulk of **Massanella**. Climbing steadily, we pass an off-path cairn-marked fork climbing on the right toward **Massanella** (Wp.12 86M) and the first fairly unimpressive - you could mistake it for a sheepfold if you didn't know what it was - snowpit (Wp.13 95M).

A second, cairn-marked off-path ascent of **Massanella** forks off to the southwest at the corner of a sharp left hand bend in the main path (Wp.14 104M), 275 metres after which we reach the Coll des Prat at a signposted junction beside a crumbling wall (Wp.15 108M). Crossing the wall and bearing left for the 'Casa de Neu d'en Galileu 1h15', we follow a narrow path marked with prominent wayposts over a band of rough rock and descend past a second more substantial snowpit.

The path, still narrow but well-defined and clearly marked with cairns or wayposts, zigzags down into the spectacular **Comafreda Valley** toward the **Coll des Telégraf**, which is flanked by a couple of really striking

Comfreda valley

snowpits, dug so deep and lined so neatly with tailored stone you begin to appreciate just how highly people used to value refrigeration for culinary and medicinal purposes.

Having enjoyed a superb outlook over **Puig Major** and the snaking progress of the celebrated **Nus de Corbata** road (the 'tie knot' since it actually tunnels under itself at one point) down to **Sa Calobra**, we turn right at the **Coll des Telégraf** (Wp.16 119M) and descend (E) past the largest snowpit yet along the right flank of the **Comafreda Valley**, enjoying fine views over the **Albufera** wetlands and **Alcúdia** bay. The path doubles back to the left a couple of hundred metres after the snow-gathering ruins and we cross the dry

Comafreda torrent (Wp.17 128M) to begin climbing toward the diminutive, but enchanting summit of **Puig d'en Galileu**. A gentle to steady climb on a rocky path cutting a swathe through the *carritx* brings us to a waypost at an intersection with a path off to the right to **Puig d'en Galileu** (Wp.18 140M). Turning left, we enjoy one of the most astonishing spectacles yet as we stroll along a broad, *carritx* covered 'balcony' overlooking the gash of the **Torrent de Pareis** (Europe's second largest gorge) and the final sweep of mountains off to the east.

The square building directly ahead of us, perched pretty much in the middle of nowhere to the right of the gorge, is the **Quartel de Carabiners**, an abandoned barrack dating back to the days when the wild northern coast with its harum-scarum *passos* was so popular with smugglers. Ignoring a minor, cairn-marked branch off to the left (Wp.19 147M), we descend (NW) to a signposted junction (Wp.20 151M) with a path accessing the well preserved 'Casa de Neu d'en Galileu'. Doubling back to the right at the junction, we head east to the edge of the **Galileu** balcony, where we reach the head of the magnificent **Camí de Ses Voltes** (Wp.21 157M), at which point the **Lluc** monastery comes into view. The path zigzags down toward the **Son Macip** wood, twisting back and forth so tightly it resembles terracing from above.

The path continues its serpentine progress as we move down through the upper reaches of the wood, where it becomes a dirt track (Wp.22 173M) that winds downhill past *sitjes* so mossy you half suspect they're part of a lovingly tended lawn or perhaps a hobgoblin's bowling green. Ignoring a branch track doubling back to the left (Wp.23 180M) then carrying straight on 200 metres later when the main track swings left (Wp.24), we follow a contour for 400 metres. The contour track then dips into a gentle slope that takes us past a picnic table, immediately after which, we turn right on a narrow, wayposted path (Wp.25 189M) going through a gate to join a charcoal burners' cart track (Wp.26 190M).

Puig Tomir

Turning left, we descend steadily to cross the MA-10 (Wp.27 197M), beyond which we follow a path (E) that soon broadens to a cart track descending gently through the woods towards **Puig Tomir**. 300 metres later, the track becomes a cobbled trail and the gradient steepens before eventually bottoming out beside a terrace path branching off to the left (Wp.28 210M).

Carrying straight on, we follow the broad, wayposted trail until it emerges at a junction with the **Camí Vell de Lluc** (climbing from **Caimari** where the island's main pilgrimage routes converge) at the southwestern corner of the **Lluc** car park, beside the **Font Cuberta** (a spring said to be an excellent curative for stomach upsets) and the restaurant of the same name (reputation unspecified) (Wp.29 216M).

The **Ca s'Amitger** bus stop is at the far end of the car park.

A long standing favourite with holidaymakers, the **Carretera Vella** between **Lluc** and **Pollença** is recommended for those who like their walking on the leisurely side. Following the remains of a cobbled trail that dates back to Roman times, we traverse lovely woodland, enjoy fine views over the **Tramuntana**'s eastern summits, and pass within a few hundred metres of some of Mallorca's most impressive karst. The walk sounds complicated, but is well signposted throughout.

2 | 4H | 15 km | 160m / 635m | one way | 4*

in Pollença

Access: by bus from **Sóller** and **Alcúdia** (L354 seasonal service), **Palma** (L330), and **Inca** (L332). The walk starts 150 metres from the **Lluc** monastery gates on the access road leading to the MA10, where there is a clearly signposted trail heading SE toward the **Son Amer** refuge (Wp.1).

Taking the **Son Amer** trail (Wp.1 0M), we pass the refuge 650 metres later (Wp.2) and descend to the refuge car park, where there is an exceptionally large oak and a 'Camina per Mallorca' mapboard (10M). Behind the oak and mapboard we take a broad trail alongside the MA10, which we cross 100 metres later (Wp.3) to continue on a new path leading to a stony track, sometimes known as the **Camí de s'Ermita**. Traversing reclaimed land recently replanted with saplings (E), we go through a gateway in a wall (Wp.4 17M). Ignoring a branch off to the left immediately after the gateway, we carry straight on along a broad track climbing gently through the woods.

The track eventually veers south to an intersection with another track, immediately before which, we turn sharp left on a narrow, wayposted path (Wp.5 27M) that traces out a dogleg round the restored, seventeenth century **Ermita de Son Amer** before rejoining the main track just above the **Font de s'Ermita** (Wp.6 33M).

Turning left, we continue climbing amid immaculately maintained oak wood, ignoring two branches off to the right and a 'Mirador' signposted branch on the left. 25 metres later, we fork right on a wayposted path (Wp.7) leading to a stile over a wall after a further 75 metres (42M).

The stile at Wp.12

Ignoring a track descending to the right immediately after the stile, we cross the plateau of **Coll Pelat** (N) to reach a junction with a dirt track 130 metres later (Wp.8). The left branch descends to the publicly owned **Menut** farmhouse, but we bear right, maintaining altitude for the moment amid marvelously mossy mature oak. After going through a gateway, the track descends within sight of the western wall of **Puig Tomir** to reach an S-bend, at the top of which a waypost indicates where we leave the track, carrying straight on along a very narrow dirt path (Wp.9 56M).

The path becomes much clearer once we're on it, contouring round the **Moleta de Binifaldó** to reach the head of the access road at the gates of the former **Binifaldó** bottling plant, where the classic ascent of **Puig Tomir** begins (see Walk 44) (Wp.10 68M). If you need water, steps lead to a spring on the right 100 metres down the access road. Otherwise, we simply follow the access road (rarely busy, closed to traffic altogether at the weekends, and even tinged with moss in places, as if the forest has a fancy to reclaim the thing) for 700 metres, bringing into view the summits of **Puig Roig** and **Puig Caragoler de Femenia**, and passing some fabulous centenary oaks.

75 metres after the **Binifaldó** farmhouse, formerly the property of the Knights Templars after they'd nabbed it off Bini Haldum (AKA the Moorish 'sons of Haldum') and now run by the government as a *Centre d'Educaci Ambiental*, we turn right on a signposted trail for 'Pollença 3h' (Wp.11 80M). We are now on the 'old road' proper, the bit that has always beguiled your more laid-back walker; frankly, it's the sort of 'road' that makes you hanker for the days when donkeys took precedence over cars and drivers who didn't employ a pedestrian with a flag to warn of their advent were considered an anti social nuisance.

After crossing the **Binifaldó** pasture, we're soon back in the woods again, much of it so mossy, one's tempted to call it mossland with a bit of wood scattered about for the purposes of decoration, though there are some outstanding mature oak.

Passing a track descending on the left to

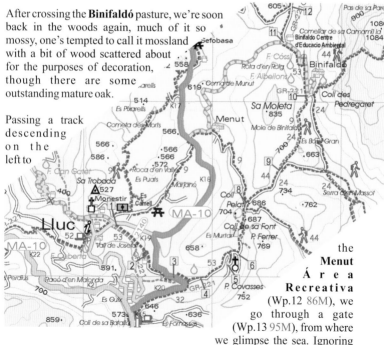

the **Menut Área Recreativa** (Wp.12 86M), we go through a gate (Wp.13 95M), from where we glimpse the sea. Ignoring all unmarked branches, we follow the main track as it descends gently, enjoying ever improving views over the bay of **Pollença** and the rugged peninsula of **Cap Formentor.**

A little under a kilometre from Wp.18, we reach our first wayposted shortcut (Wp.14 104M), a restored stretch of the old cobbled trail re-crossing the track less than 50 metres later.

The descent steepens as we zigzag down beside the **Font de Muntanya** torrent (an ideal spot for a picnic), which we cross via a solitary stepping stone, immediately after which we rejoin the track (Wp.15 110M).

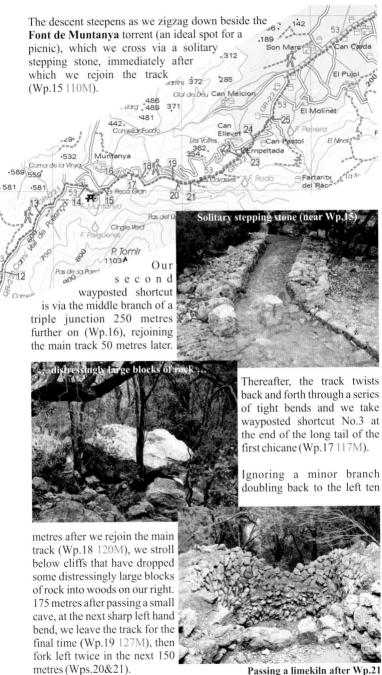

Solitary stepping stone (near Wp.15)

...distressingly large blocks of rock...

Our second wayposted shortcut is via the middle branch of a triple junction 250 metres further on (Wp.16), rejoining the main track 50 metres later.

Thereafter, the track twists back and forth through a series of tight bends and we take wayposted shortcut No.3 at the end of the long tail of the first chicane (Wp.17 117M).

Ignoring a minor branch doubling back to the left ten metres after we rejoin the main track (Wp.18 120M), we stroll below cliffs that have dropped some distressingly large blocks of rock into woods on our right. 175 metres after passing a small cave, at the next sharp left hand bend, we leave the track for the final time (Wp.19 127M), then fork left twice in the next 150 metres (Wps.20&21).

Passing a limekiln after Wp.21

Karst in the Son Marc valley

After a serpentine descent through a stretch of woodland so deep and dense and steep, it's almost like we're spiralling into some pit at the bottom of the world, the gradient eases as we pass a limekiln. 75 metres later, we fork right at a Y junction (Wp.22 145M), then turn right

50 metres after that (Wp.23) to follow a new fence down to cross the end of the lane that climbs the **Son Marc** valley (Wp.24 149M). The path rejoins the lane 300 metres later (Wp.25 154M), at which point we simply bear left and follow the lane all the way to the MA10.

Torrent de la Vall d'en Marc

When the lane joins the MA10 (Wp.26 186M), we bear right and follow a scruffy path running parallel to the road alongside the **Torrent de la Vall d'en Marc**. Road and walking trail diverge 400 metres later, 50 metres after which we ignore a track crossing a bridge on our right for the 'Vall de Pollença Agroturisme' (Wp.27) and continue along the left bank of the torrent.

350 metres later, the path has been washed away, so we clamber onto the wall on our left where it broadens to a raised stone-clad 'road' (Wp.28 201M), then promptly descend to cross a dirt track beside a bridge, after which we continue our pleasant riverside stroll.

Karst on the Serra d'en Massot

Bypassing a fence (a remnant of the days when this route was contested), we traverse a patch of eroded river bank via some wonderfully haphazard wooden steps, shortly after which we cross a dirt track beside a ford.

350 metres later, we reach a ford across an affluent (Wp.29 212M) and turn left to join the MA10, which we follow to the right (on a path but cheek by jowl with the road) for 600 metres.

... haphazard wooden steps ...

At the km2.8 metre stone (Wp.30 222M), we take a dirt track that shadows the road before joining a lane a little under 100 metres later.

Ponta Roma refuge

The lane swings right after 175 metres, at which point we carry straight on along a dirt track (Wp.31 225M). When the track dips down into a ford, we cross a new footbridge and turn left on a broad lane (Wp.32), which we follow for a kilometre until it arrives in **Pollença** beside the **Pont Roma** refuge (Wp.33 235M).

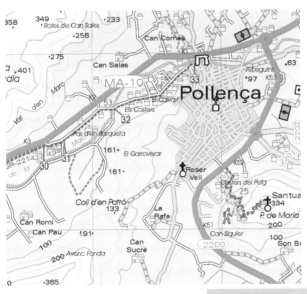

This glossary contains Spanish and Catalán words found in the text (shown in *italics*) plus other local words that you may encounter. Please note that the spelling of place names and other local words on signs and maps can vary according to local conventions.

SPANISH	**CATALÁN**	
a		
agua, con/sin gas		water, fizzy/still
aljibe	**aljub**	ancient cistern/reservoir
alto	**dalt**	high, upper
área recreativa		picnic spot, usually with barbecues, toilets, water
atalaya		ancient watch-tower
avenida	**avinguda**	avenue
ayuntamiento	**ayuntament**	town hall
b		
bajo	**baix**	low
bajo	**avall**	lower
barranco	**barranc**	gorge, ravine
botadores		stone steps in country walls
c		
cala		creek, small bay, sometimes just a tiny coastal indentation
cala		inlet, cove
calle	**carrer**	street
camino	**camí**	road, path or way
camino real	**camí real**	royal road, once a major donkey trail
campo		countryside, field
canaleta	**siquia**	man-made water channel, including anything from a concrete canal to delicately arched aqueducts
carritx		pampas-like grass
casa	**can/ca**	house of (as *chez* in French)
casa de nieve	**casa neu**	snow pit/ice house
caseta		hut, cabin, small house
cingles		cliffs, crags; most often used to describe the sort of short, abrupt cliffs that typically define the rounded summits of many Catalán and Mallorcan mountains
ciudad	**ciutat**	city
coll		saddle, neck or pass
correos		post office
costa		coast
e		
embalse		reservoir
ermita		hermitage, small church, shrine
f		
faro		lighthouse
fiesta		festival, public holiday
finca	**lluc**	farm
forn de calc	**horno de calç**	lime kiln
fuente	**font**	spring, well
l		
lavadero		public laundry area
llano	**pla**	plain, flat land
m		
medio	**mig**	middle
mercado	**mercat**	market

mirador		viewing point, sometimes with man-made facilities, more often a natural place with a good view
morro		snout or muzzle, a rounded summit

p

parada		bus stop
particular		private
paseo	***passeig***	walkway
peatones		pedestrians
peña	***penya/penyal***	rock or boulder, used for a knoll or pinnacle on a ridge
pico	***puig***	translates as 'hill' or 'height', though more often a peak or mountain
pista		dirt road
pista forestal		forest road
playa	***platja***	beach
plaza	***plaça***	town square
pozo	***pou***	well
privado		private
prohibido el paso		no entry
puerto	***port***	port, mountain pass

r

refugio		mountain refuge, some offering basic overnight accommodation

s

santo/a	***san/sant***	saint
santuario	***santuari***	monastery, hermitage
sendero	***senda***	footpath, trail
sitja (pl. sitjes)	***sitja***	charcoal burning area or circle
su	***son, sa, ses***	his, her, their

t

tipico		typical, locals' café/bar
toro bravo		wild bull
torre		tower, often a coastal watchtower built to warn of approaching pirates, or a Moorish lookout tower
torrente	***torrent***	stream

u

urbanización		housing development

ON THE MAP

See the notes in the introduction on page 13. If you are using an earlier edition Tour & Trail Map, the following list cross-references walking route numbers in this book, with walk numbers in previous publications.

W refers to Walk! Mallorca West, **N&M** refers to Walk! Mallorca North & Mountains, **Stage** refers to GR221, Mallorca's Dry Stone Way.

1	W2 Calvià: Mirador de n'Alzamora
2	N&M 9 Sóller - Port de Sóller
3	N&M 33b Campanet: Font des Ufanes
4	N&M 28 Port de Pollença: The Siller Pass
5	W1 Calvià: Pujol des Gats
6	N&M 11 Port de Sóller: The Ultimate PicnicWalk - Torre Picada & Sa Illeta
7	N&M 12 Sóller: Capelleta & Campo
8	N&M 22a Sa Calobra: The Torrent de Pareis
9	N&M 29 Lluc: Binifaldó
10	N&M 34 Mortitx: L'Havanor

Please note that the spelling of place names and other local words on signs and maps can vary according to local conventions; Castilian and Mallorquin versions are frequently different..